nps. gov/shen

MW00669091

Scavenger
SHENANDOAH NATIONAL PARK
Hike
Adventures

By Kat and John LaFevre
llustrations by G Webb

Bring walking sticks.

4/15/2021 Skyland Resort

slippers for cold feet in room

Ranger-led 2.5hr. Tours to Rapidan Camp
start from Harry F Byrd V.C. - online or
Reserv. 540-999-3283
↳ Recreation.gov 10:00Am - midnight EST
877 444-6777 special Tours
6mo in advance

Scavenger Hike Adventures

SHENANDOAH NATIONAL PARK

Handwritten: April 17-21 Nat Pk Wk.

Handwritten: P 109   LV

Front Royal

⑫ Pioneer Farm

Dickey Ridge Area

Handwritten: 44.7

⑪ *Handwritten:* visitor ctr. / mi 21

⑩

Handwritten: thorn

Handwritten: gas [mile 51 / Big Meadows Wayside]

Stand on 2nd Highest Peak ①

⑬

Handwritten: #1

Handwritten: 38.6 / See Spring / 1 Mary's Head / off / Hughes River Camp

⑧ *Handwritten:* P 31

47.1
Skyland Area

2nd Highest Waterfall ⑤

③

④

To Highest Mountain Peak

Handwritten: Visitor Ctr.   51.

Big Meadows Area

Handwritten: ? ✗
President Hoover's Hidden Cabin Retreat

⑨

Old Copper Mine

60

Watch for 3 Huge Waterfalls ⑥

Loft Mountain Area

⑦ *Handwritten:* 84.5 / Blackrock / Summit / P 58

80

⑭

100

Legend

- ▢ Shenandoah National Park
- — Skyline Drive
- △ Milepost
- ⍟ Scavenger Hike Adventures

wildflowers spring. South River
Hughs River
Rose River
Mill Prong.

Later. Skyline Drive & Big Meadows

Scavenger Hike Adventures   Fall colors 2-3wk Oct.
Treasure Map Key

Find over 200 hidden Natural and Historic "Treasures"

Yes ✓ **1** Stony Man Trail to the Summit – MILE 41.7   1.6 mi long easy!

✓ **2** Mill Prong Trail to President Hoover's   3.6 mi long moderate
Hidden Cabin and Rapidan Camp – MILE 52.8

③ The Limberlost Trail – MILEPOST 43   1.3 mi easy

4 Hawksbill Summit Via the AT & Salamander Trail – MILE 45.6   86' water
4 hrs.   4.8 mi fall long

5 Whiteoak Canyon Trail to the First Waterfall – MILE 42.6
6.6 mi

6 Browns Gap Trail Loop to Upper & Lower Doyles River Falls &
Jones Run Falls & Return Via Appalachian Trail – MILEPOST 83   1 mile 1 hour

258' ✗ **⑦** Blackrock Summit Loop – MILE 84.8   6.8 mi extreme   1 mile loop. 45 min +175'
incredible views

8 Jewell Hollow Overlook to Marys Rock Summit – MILE 36.4   4. 4-5 hrs. mod, hills

✗ **9** Rose River Falls Loop to Rose River Falls   2.2
& Dark Hollow Falls – MILE 49.4   but steep & rocky

✗ **10** Compton Peak – MILE 10.4   extreme   or extreme?

⑪ Sugarloaf Loop – MILEPOST 21   1 mi, 1 hr easy

Yes **12** Fox Hollow Trail – MILE 4.6   easy 2 mi   1½ hrs View

? **13** Appalachian Trail Ridge Hike – MILE 36.7   sheer drops   mod 2 mi
easy

14 Riprap Trail to Calvary Rocks & Chimney Rock – MILEPOST 90

THIS BOOK IS DEDICATED to my mother, Irma, whose positive attitude along with her love and zest for life has been an inspiration to many. She has conquered many obstacles with her courage and determination and lives each day appreciating, enjoying, and savoring its every moment.

Kat

SCAVENGER HIKE ADVENTURES

"Don't **Just** Take a Hike…
Take a Scavenger Hike Adventure!!!"

Contents

SCAVENGER HIKE ADVENTURES

4/15/2002 wonderful

save turn out sign

midtones missed

About This Unique Hiking Guide!

Scavenger Hike Adventures is an *interactive* hiking guide series for all levels of hikers! **Hikers have fun following clues** on national park trails **to find hidden natural and historic treasures!** One mountain hiking guide commented that the book *is like having a pioneer settler and a mountain explorer hiking along with you!*

Ten points are earned for each "treasure" found and hikers **earn an official achievement certificate** for each completed trail! Certificates suitable for framing can be found at **scavengerhikeadventures.com.**

A **group leader** should carry the book and **read the clues out loud** as the hiking expedition searches for the treasures.

No longer is a hike simply from the trailhead to some destination miles and hours away. In a Scavenger Hike Adventure your destination is the next treasure that you discover just . . . "36 steps past the next log footbridge."

Debbie N. from Indianapolis, Indiana, may have said it best:
"This book gives a new meaning to hiking!"

"Don't **Just** Take a Hike… Take a Scavenger Hike Adventure!!!"

Kat and John can be reached at *scavengerhike@aol.com.* They welcome suggestions or comments and are available for entertaining and inspirational corporate and group presentations.

What Is a Scavenger Hike Adventure . . . Anyway?

The beautiful Blue Ridge Mountains are calling! Grab your family or friend! **An exciting and fun wilderness adventure is waiting for you!**

Scavenger Hike Adventures are challenging and **great fun for amateur hikers, experienced day hikers, and serious trekkers!** Hikes range from an easy 1-mile level trek to a challenging extreme adventure that passes 3 awesome waterfalls on a combination of trails . . . and adventures that lead to 4 of the highest peaks in the park!

Five Scavenger Hike Adventures are kind of **Easy** for all ages and skill levels, 6 are **Moderate** or challenging, and 3 are **Extreme** or strenuous . . . and will probably make you breathe hard! All 14 hikes lead to exciting discoveries!

Are you up for the challenge? Follow our clues and find . . . 5 awesome waterfalls . . . a bird that dives 200 miles per hour . . . a hidden presidential camp used by 2 U.S. presidents and 2 vice-presidents . . . remains of an **abandoned copper mine . . .** an unusual **telescope tree . . .** 4 of the **highest peaks in the national park . . .** a single **Civil War gravestone** hidden alone in the wild . . . a giant **truck-sized boulder balancing on another rock . . .** and **over 200 other unusual treasures!**

Earn 10 points for each treasure that you find and achieve 1 of 3 certificate levels! Finally answer the question:

Are you a . . .? City Slicker! Pioneer Scout!! or Frontier Explorer!!!

"Don't **Just** Take a Hike... Take a Scavenger Hike Adventure!!!"

SHENANDOAH NATIONAL PARK

"Beauty Beyond Description!"
It has been said that the Indian word "Shenandoah" means "Daughter of the Stars." There are no words or photographs that can capture the park's magnificent beauty.

There is an incredible breathtaking moment waiting for you around every curve of the 105-mile-long Skyline Drive. George Freeman Pollock, owner and manager of historic Skyland Resort, used just three words—"Beauty Beyond Description!"— for this incredible place following his first visit here in the late 1800s.

There is truly only one way to *feel the magic* of a Shenandoah sunset as colored beams of light paint the sky behind layers upon layers of blue misty mountains . . . or to *sense the wonder* as a doe and her fawn stroll together through a flower-filled meadow.

YOU MUST EXPERIENCE IT!

Please remember that you are entering a *very fragile and diverse system* of plants, water, and animals that is *known and cherished throughout the world.* There are over 50 different kinds of mammals, 200 kinds of birds, 100 different species of trees, and over 1200 different plants in Shenandoah National Park. Forty percent of this truly amazing national park is officially designated as "wilderness" and 101 miles of the famous hiking trail, the Appalachian National Scenic Trail (AT), that stretches for over 2,175 miles from Springer Mountain, Georgia, to Mount Katahdin, Maine, winds directly through Shenandoah National Park! It is all ours to enjoy!

Three words *do* perfectly describe Shenandoah National Park . . . .
"Beauty Beyond Description!"

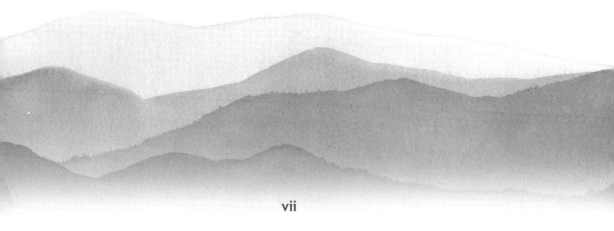

Who Are Your Scavenger Hike Adventure Guides?

Kat and John LaFevre are avid hikers in our national parks and are **authors of a new, fun, and exciting hiking book series called Scavenger Hike Adventures.** They live in a rural mountain log cabin and spend many months each year hiking and researching the hidden treasures on awesome trails in our national parks. They have researched, hiked, and explored Shenandoah National Park with local experts and national park rangers to discover the hidden *natural* and *historic* treasures in Shenandoah.

Kat has a bachelor and master's degree in elementary education, taught for several years, and has assisted in national park Outreach Programs. Kat often closes her presentations with a favorite quote:

"Life is not measured by the number of breaths you take, but instead . . . by the number of times your breath is taken away."
(G. Carlin)

John majored in English and Communications and is a business consultant and professional speaker. He has written feature articles for the *Wall Street Journal's National Employment Weekly*, the *College Placement Annual,* and many other national magazines. He is especially proud that his backcountry barbeque (while serving as a Sherpa for a magazine writer) was mentioned in *National Geographic Magazine*.

He has also written a business book published by Simon & Schuster, issued in three editions. John is a country musician and songwriter when he is not out on the trails or talkin' somewhere.

You can reach Kat and John directly at *Scavengerhike@aol.com*

"Kat and John invite you to have fun!"

Our Thanks!

Our thanks to the wonderful park rangers, volunteers, and professional employees of Shenandoah National Park for the outreach programs, ranger-led hikes, and special evening programs at Skyland and Big Meadows resorts. They were invaluable resources as we researched the hidden treasures in the park.

In particular, special thanks to Karen Michaud, Chief of Interpretation and Education, and Greta Miller, Executive Director of the Shenandoah National Park Association. They reviewed our drafts and offered invaluable insight, guidance, and encouragement from start to finish. We are fortunate to have them working for all of us in our national park.

Thanks to park rangers Sally Hurlbert, Jerry Dofflemyer, Mara Meisel, and Debbie Caro for their continuous help throughout the research process. Joy Lorien, a long-time employee of Skyland Resort, inspired us with her great love for Shenandoah National Park.

A special thanks to Helen Morton, Director of Sales and Marketing, ARAMARK Shenandoah National Park, and the entire Skyland Resort and Big Meadows Lodge staff. For our many Indonesian friends working as staff at the resorts, "terima kasih."

Thanks to our friends Mark and Macaroni Clark who helped field-test the trails and helped research "treasures." Thanks to Kevin and Amy Van De Water and Lori LaFevre for their continual support.

Skyline Drive!

"A High-Way in the Sky"

What a road! Each year about 2 million people experience the **awesome 105-mile-long Skyline Drive**. It was built along the crest of the **Blue Ridge Mountains** and winds through the heart of Shenandoah National Park in Virginia. It is like driving in the "sky"! There are **75 overlooks** where you can pull off the road and enjoy the stunning vistas! Most of the **500-plus miles of hiking trails** in Shenandoah National Park start at a point somewhere along the Skyline Drive. What a road!

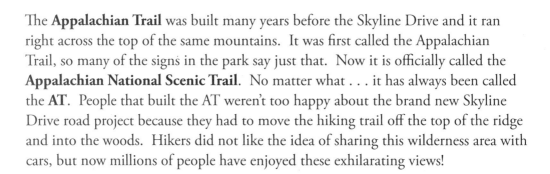

In 1930 **President Hoover** rode his horse up to the ridge of these mountains from his cabin down by the Rapidan River. He looked around and turned to the National Park Service Director and said, **"These mountains were just made for a highway. I think everybody ought to have the chance to get the views from here!"** It took thousands of workers and the joint efforts of the state and federal government to make this road happen. What an amazing project! The **Skyline Drive was built in sections between 1931 and 1937.**

The **Appalachian Trail** was built many years before the Skyline Drive and it ran right across the top of the same mountains. It was first called the Appalachian Trail, so many of the signs in the park say just that. Now it is officially called the **Appalachian National Scenic Trail**. No matter what . . . it has always been called the **AT**. People that built the AT weren't too happy about the brand new Skyline Drive road project because they had to move the hiking trail off the top of the ridge and into the woods. Hikers did not like the idea of sharing this wilderness area with cars, but now millions of people have enjoyed these exhilarating views!

Just hop on the amazing Skyline Drive and you will know one thing for sure . . .

THE JOURNEY IS THE DESTINATION!

The Wildlife is . . . Wild and Wonderful!!!

If you like wildlife . . . you will *love* the Shenandoah National Park! There are **over 50 species of mammals** in the park and **over 200 kinds of birds.** There are **300-500 black bears** and **thousands of white-tailed deer!** Some of our other favorites are chipmunks, wild turkeys, butterflies, squirrels, raccoons, turkey vultures, peregrine falcons, and salamanders!

Tips For Watching Wildlife

Remember, you are watching them, not interacting with them! If an animal changes its behavior by stopping its grazing, looking up and staring at you, or running away because of you . . . you are way too close! It's kind of like if a bear came into your living room and sat in your favorite easy chair while you were getting a snack out of the fridge or if a family of raccoons walked into your bathroom while you were showering . . . it would change *your* behavior. ***Don't get so close that an animal changes its behavior!***

Obey all national park signs regarding wildlife.

Don't block traffic.

Don't ever shine spotlights, flashlights, or your car's headlights on an animal.

Don't feed animals granola bars, trail mix, peanuts, sour cream & onion chips . . . or anything! It can make them very sick. Don't love 'em to death.

Animals are called "wildlife" for a reason. Enjoy wildlife from a distance!

SPECIAL NOTE ABOUT ALL THOSE BEAUTIFUL WHITE-TAILED DEER:

Deer love to snack and hang out on the fringes or edges of forests. The Skyline Drive usually has grass and other favorite deer snacks growing on each side. . . so you can almost always find deer along the road. **Please always observe the speed limit of no more than 35 m.p.h.** There could be a deer in the middle of the road around that next curve. (*The deer asked us to specifically mention this! They also said, "Thanks."*)

BABY FAWNS: You will most likely see many baby fawns in the spring and summer in Shenandoah National Park. At times you just **might see them** *lying very still* **all alone.** The mother is not far away and a fawn does this to protect itself from prey. **Never touch a baby fawn!** Remember to always observe it from a distance.

Lions and Tigers and Bears, OH MY!

You can rest easy . . . there are no lions or tigers in Shenandoah National Park! There *are* about **300-500 black bears** and it is very important to be aware of these wild animals. They are very strong and powerful and *can* **become dangerous.** The national park visitor centers have published safety guidelines and you should review them carefully. **Always respect all wild animals in the wilderness.** When a bear is born it is about the size of a can of soda pop. It has no fur. . . but already has claws! A bear can run 30 miles per hour and can climb up and down trees in seconds. Here are some important bear tips:

Hike in groups and never let your children run ahead or separate from you. **Always stay together with your Scavenger Hike Adventure exploration party!**

If you see a bear, remain watchful, stay calm, and **do not approach it!** Pick up small children!

NEVER EVER RUN OR TURN YOUR BACK ON A BEAR!

Slowly back away, stand on a rock, raise your arms to look bigger, and **gather close together with your hiking group.**

Most bears want to avoid a confrontation with you. **Give them plenty of room** and a way to escape from you**. REMEMBER . . . ALWAYS BACK AWAY.**

If a **bear persists in following you, speak to it firmly in a loud voice, clap your hands,** and **make noise.**

If attacked, **fight back. Do not play dead!**

What's All This Talk About Rumpledumps?

For most visitors, your experience in Shenandoah National Park is going to be just one wonderful breathtaking moment after another! But . . . there is **a very tiny little bug you need to know about**. Like mosquitos and other insects, it can carry disease. Here is a "fun" Scavenger Hike Adventure clue:

Its name sounds identical to the first syllable in "**tic**-tac-toe" . . . the first syllable of the word "**tic**kle" . . . and the first word in "**tic** tac paddywack give a dog a bone." We really don't like the name of this bug (**"ick" with a "t" in front**), so we call them **"rumpledumps."**

Rumpledumps can't jump or fly. They hold on to leaves and grass and bushes until they detect heat or chemicals from the body or breath of an animal or hiker. Then they wave their tiny little arms and legs around to **try to latch on to you** as you pass by. These rumpledumps then might give a tiny bite to hold onto your leg or neck or arm or head. Since you can't hold your breath or keep your body cold, what can you do to avoid rumpledumps???

How to avoid rumpledumps:
- Wear long pants and long sleeves. **Stay on the trail.**
- In heavy high grassy areas like Big Meadows **tuck your hiking pants into your socks.**
- Wear **a hat**.
- Use insect repellent with the chemical **"deet"** in it.

How do you get a rumpledump off you or your dog or child?
- Use **tweezers** to pull it off.
- If you don't have tweezers, **slide a credit card** up against it and pull it off.
- Be sure to **remove** any remaining parts **with a sterile needle.**

When you shower at the end of the day, remind your friends, **"Hey, be sure to check for rumpledumps!"** And that's all we have to say about that.

Lightning and Falling Trees!

Caution! Be Careful!

Without getting real complicated . . . **here is how lightning "happens."** Clouds can generate a negative charge (like the negative side of a flashlight battery) and send invisible negative (what scientists call) *"leaders"* down toward the ground. Picture those invisible long wavy lines coming down toward the hiking trail from a cloud. Those invisible lines can actually travel miles from the cloud. Meanwhile, a tree or a mountain top or a PERSON like you has a *positive* charge and if that invisible negative leader from the cloud gets close enough . . . it will create a path for the lightning and come crashing down. That is why you should **never put you or your family in a situation during a storm where the tallest thing around you . . . is YOU!**

Lightning Fast Facts

Lightning is **very serious and dangerous.** Did you know that a lightning bolt is hotter than the temperature on the surface of the sun?

Thunderstorms can roll into Shenandoah **anytime during the spring and summer months.**

When that lightning bolt gets created it rapidly heats up the air around it and complicated scientific things happen that create thunder. There is not a question about which comes first . . . lightning or thunder. **If you hear thunder, there absolutely was lightning!** If someone says to you, "It is *only* thundering and I don't see any lightning," then you answer back, "Lightning created that thunder." **Lightning can occur many miles away from the storm cloud** you see in the distance.

IF YOU HEAR THUNDER . . . IT IS TIME TO BE GETTING TO SAFETY.

Lightning Safety Tips

- Avoid peaks and ridges.
- You are **safer in a forest** than standing near a lone tree or high object.
- **Stay away from trunks of trees** even in the forest.
- **Cliffs, caves, or overhanging rock arches** are **especially dangerous.**
- **Boulders and rocks can conduct electricity.** Avoid sitting or leaning on them.
- **Metal fences, bridges, and metal towers are lightning "magnets."**

Falling Trees

There are **many dead trees** in Shenandoah National Park **because of insects, tree diseases, strong winds, ice storms, and landslides.** Always be aware when you are near standing dead trees especially during periods of **high winds**.

SCAVENGER HIKE ADVENTURES

Top 10 Day Hiker Checklist

1 Always protect Shenandoah National Park! Treat it like the "treasure" that it is! **DON'T PICK ANYTHING! DON'T TAKE ANYTHING! DON'T LEAVE ANYTHING!**

2 **Stay on the trails!** Respect and protect each and every plant and animal in the park!

3 Don't forget to **pack your common sense.** This is a wilderness area!

4 **Water is the most important item for you to bring! Never drink from streams and rivers!**

5 **Bring snacks or lunch along!** Food tastes at least twice as good in the woods! *walking sticks!*

6 Always plan on some raindrops falling on your head! **Bring a poncho!** Forget the weather forecast . . . be prepared for *surprise* rain and wind!

7 **Insect repellent** is a handy item especially in the summer!

○ extra socks - if get wet

8 **Hiking boots are great! Gym shoes are fine.** Sandals are not recommended. Wear flip-flops and that is just what you will do!
WHEN COUNTING STEPS TO FIND TREASURES . . . SMALL FOLKS TAKE TALL STEPS AND TALL FOLKS TAKE SMALL STEPS!

9 **Wet rocks and roots can be very slippery!** Please watch your step! Be especially **careful around waterfalls!** Hiking sticks are pretty cool and really will help with balance.

10 Most hikers who have gotten lost . . . separated and went ahead of their group! **Stay with your exploration party** and have a great Scavenger Hike Adventure!

4,010 *wonderfull* (handwritten)

Stony Man Trail to the Summit

1

Scavenger Hike Adventure

EASY
1.6 MILES ROUNDTRIP
1-2 HOURS

Why This is a Great Trail! This easy and exciting *high altitude* Scavenger Hike Adventure leads you to the **second highest mountain summit** in all of Shenandoah National Park! The mountain called **Stony Man** is shaped just like a bearded man's face and *you will actually stand on his rocky "forehead" at 4,010 feet elevation!* Whew! The views will blow you away! On this Scavenger Hike Adventure you will find **incredible shrinking trees**, a **40-mile-long mountain**, a **gray ghost,** and the site of an **old copper mine!** You will hike on the world-famous **Appalachian Trail!** On the peak of Stony Man Mountain you will search for a **bird that flies as fast as a NASCAR race car** and captures its food in mid-air! You will enjoy the "bird's-eye" views from Stony Man peak and you will soar above the mountains without even having to leave the ground! Wow!!!

Where's the Trail? The trailhead is located in the Central District of the park at **mile 41.7** just after you turn into the *north* entrance to Skyland Resort. There is a large parking lot for about 40 cars on the right (north) side of the entrance road.

About the Trail: This is an **EASY** trail with a few short steep sections, but is do-able for all ages of explorers. There are a few rocky sections and the summit is a large area of exposed rock. *There are some sheer drops at the* only *peak. Watch the kids! Remember that wet rocks are very slippery.* You'll get a peaceful, easy feelin' at the top of Stony Man Mountain!

How Long is This Hike? This Scavenger Hike Adventure is **1.6 miles roundtrip** and will **take between 1 and 2 hours** allowing plenty of time to relax and to enjoy the views from the summit! *us 2hrs* (handwritten)

STOP! WHOA! HOLD IT!
DO NOT PROCEED TO THE TRAILHEAD
UNTIL YOU READ CLUE #1.

at parking for trailhead

Things To Hunt For

(Earn 10 points for each treasure you find.)

❶ Find Stony Man!

Before you begin your hike, drive on the ~~Skyline Drive~~ to the sign for Stony Man Overlook at **mile 38.6**. It is also called **Hughes River Gap.** Go to the information sign for Stony Man. SPECIAL HINT: At this overlook you will see the **outline of Stony Man with his eyes, nose, mouth, and beard.** Take a close look and **find his forehead!** That is where *you will be standing* in just a little while! Pretty awesome, huh? Now that you have seen your destination it is time for the journey! Follow the directions to the trailhead. Then . . . on to the forehead!!!

SPECIAL NOTE: TURN RIGHT (SOUTH) AS YOU LEAVE THE OVERLOOK AND HEAD TO MILE 41.7 TO BEGIN YOUR HIKE!

10 POINTS

❷ Find the White & Blue Blazes!

(Count 5 steps to the right of the trailhead sign.) SPECIAL HINT: The blue rectangle (called a "blue blaze") painted on the tree means that this is an official Shenandoah National Park trail for hikers! **White rectangles** (called a "white blaze") mark the **Appalachian Trail!** The world-famous Appalachian Trail (AT) stretches for about **2,175 miles** from Springer Mountain, Georgia, all the way to Mt. Katahdin (pronounced "kuh-TAH-din") in Maine!

blue Shenandoah !
vertical

white! AT

10 POINTS

also cement 3'

mileposts

sometimes both

❸
Find a Thru-Hiker!

Yup ✓

_____
10 POINTS

(Along the Appalachian Trail)
SPECIAL HINT: A **thru-hiker** is a person who has decided to hike the **entire AT.** Yes, all 2,175 miles! Amazing!!! A thru-hiker usually starts the hike in April down at Springer Mountain and then finishes in September! Six months in the woods! What an adventure! Look for hikers carrying giant backpacks and wearing clothing that is searching for a washer and a dryer! If you are lucky enough to find one, be sure to ask for the thru-hiker's *special trail name*. Each thru-hiker has a very unique nickname that is usually "given" by other hikers! **Here are a few actual trail names: Hiking Pole, Ping, Pong, April Moon, Mother Goose, and Mountain Laurel.** What would *your* trail name be?

nope not in April

❹
Find Zillions of Giant Ferns!

_____
10 POINTS

(On both sides of the trail)
SPECIAL HINT: These beautiful giant **cinnamon ferns** grow to over 4 feet tall! They are huge! The **ruffed grouse**, a common bird in Shenandoah National Park, loves to snack on the cinnamon fern! **Hummingbirds** like to use the incredibly soft fern to line their nests! Hmmmmmm!

✓
❺
Find the Yellow Birch Tree Sandwich!

yup

_____
10 POINTS

(On the right---by marker #4---a tree is growing inside a cracked boulder.)
SPECIAL HINT: Check out this amazing "tree" sandwich! A long time ago a tiny seed fell into a small bit of soil in a crack in this boulder. As this **yellow birch** tree grew it broke open the boulder! By the way, look up high on the trunk. Find the **bark that looks just like shredded paper.** Indians and pioneers really appreciated this tree! It has **oil in the shredded bark** and they would use it to start a fire when all the wood in the forest was wet. This is just one awesome tree!

sat on it! 6

Find the Tree Bench!

_____
10 POINTS

(Count 70 steps from the Birch Tree Sandwich---
on the right of the trail.)
SPECIAL HINT: This tree branch has grown
sideways instead of up to the sky. Wow!
Amazing! It is quite incredible!

ok

❼

Find the Skinny Forest!

_____
10 POINTS

(On both sides of the trail---as the mountain gets steeper---just
past marker #5)
SPECIAL HINT: Find the skinny trees all around you! This
land was once *cleared* **by loggers and farmers.** Pioneers had
farms all around this area before it became a national park. The
forest that has grown back is called a **"second growth forest."**
Most of the trees are skinny because they are
fairly young. Look up to the very top
of one of the tallest trees you see!
Wow! Some of these trees are really
up there!

❽

Find the Horned Tree!

ok

_____
10 POINTS

(Count 37 steps past marker
#6---on the left of the trail---
across from the bench.)
SPECIAL HINT: This tree
looks like it has horns . . . but
actually the **lower branches** of
this white pine tree **broke off**
all on their own! This used to
be a very shady forest with huge
chestnut trees and giant hemlock
trees blocking out the sunlight.
This tree's **lower branches could
not get enough sun to grow** so
they just broke off. The sun's
energy now shines down on
the upper branches and this
tree is healthy and happy
and growing toward the sky.

9

Find the Double White Blaze Where You Must Make an Important Decision!

_____
10 POINTS

(On a tree---just a few steps before the next trail intersection)
SPECIAL HINT: **The double white** (not blue and white) **blaze** (rectangle) means the **AT is changing direction ahead**. If you decide to go to the right at this intersection . . . in _a few months_ you will arrive in Maine! If you **go straight you will arrive at the summit of Stony Man** in _a few minutes_. The decision is yours!

10

Find Bear & Turkey Food!

I'd call it big because bare of leaves in April

_____
10 POINTS

(Just before marker #10--on the right)
SPECIAL HINT:
Look on the ground for small pieces or whole acorns from this humongous **oak tree**. Bears and turkeys have something in common besides the fact that neither one of them can fly very well! They both enjoy eating **acorns**! By the way, the big "bumps" on this oak tree are caused by **"a fungus."** Find the top of this oak tree and make a mental note about how tall it is**. Shrinking trees ahead!!!**

11

Find the Blue Blaze on a Tree with 3 Trunks!

_____
10 POINTS

(At the "Y" in the trail)
SPECIAL HINT: Take the right fork in the trail and keep following the blue blazes (rectangles) to Stony Man summit. **That "forehead" you are searching for? Straight ahead!**

⑫

Find Something to Your Likin'!

10 POINTS

(Count 9 steps past marker #11---on the left of the trail.)

SPECIAL HINT: **Lichen (pronounced LIKE-in)** is a combination of **fungus and algae** and is growing on these boulders. There are hundreds of different kinds of lichen. Doesn't this one look like light green flaking paint? Lichens can live for thousands of years! When the lichen gets wet it makes an **acid** that will gradually **eat away at the rocks and turn them into soil**. Lichens can be all colors of the rainbow! REMEMBER . . . NEVER PICK OR HARM ANY PLANT OR LICHEN. HELP PROTECT SHENANDOAH NATIONAL PARK!

⑬

Find the Incredible Shrinking Trees!

10 POINTS

(In every direction---near marker #13)

SPECIAL HINT: Honey, who shrunk the trees? Are you getting taller or are the trees getting smaller? The **weather is really harsh** at this **higher elevation** and the trees figured out they could survive better if they were shorter and stayed closer to the ground where it is usually warmer and not as windy. Good plan!

⑭

Find the Amazing Gray Ghost!

10 POINTS

(Count 42 steps past marker #13---on the left.)

SPECIAL HINT: Dead **American chestnut tree stumps** and other tall dead tree stumps often turn gray and in the moonlight pioneers thought they looked like **"gray ghosts."** This forest used to be filled with huge chestnut trees but now it only has a few "gray ghosts" instead! In the **early 1900s a blight** (disease) from Asia **killed all the mature chestnut trees.**

15
Find the Copper Mine & Some Copper!

10 POINTS

(Count 13 steps back from marker #14---go to the left 10 steps on the side path.)
SPECIAL HINT: Look on the ground for **rocks** with streaks of **turquoise and green**! This area was mined for this colored mineral called **"copper."** **George H. Pollock** owned this mine and once asked his 16-year-old son to come and take a look. The mine didn't really work out, but young **George F. Pollock** fell in love with this area which he described as **"beauty beyond description!"** He thought this area was just perfect for a beautiful resort. He became an owner/manager of Skyland Resort in the late 1800s. He played an important role in helping set aside this area and getting it protected as a national park.
REMEMBER . . . ALL ROCKS ARE PROTECTED IN OUR NATIONAL PARKS.

16
Find the Summit of Stony Man Mountain!

10 POINTS

(Straight ahead)
SPECIAL HINT: You are standing on **Stony Man's forehead** at **4,010 feet** above sea level. Find Shenandoah Valley about 3,000 feet . . . below your feet! The **boulders** around you are **over 550 million years old** . . . give or take a few years . . . and were formed when lava flowed in this area. Technically speaking, this lava rock was squashed under an ocean and the high pressure and even more heat turned it into what you are standing on today—**greenstone.**
CAUTION: DANGEROUS DROP-OFFS AHEAD

17
Find Skyland Resort!

WS Rm
115 handicapped

_____
10 POINTS

(Look straight out---then push your chin as much as you can to the left.)

SPECIAL HINT: **Skyland Resort** was a great place to stay over 100 years ago . . . and still is today! It was first called **"Stony Man Camp."** City folks from Baltimore, Philadelphia, and Washington, D.C., came here to escape the heat and the hustle and bustle of the cities. Hey! George Pollock's picture is still hanging up over the fireplace at Skyland Resort and the views from the rooms will help you understand why he built the resort on this spot. Skyland is a beautiful rustic resort filled with history. Even if you don't stay at Skyland Resort, it is definitely worth a look! A tour of **Massanutten Lodge**, where George and his wife Addie lived, is well worth your time!

18
Find a 40-Mile-Long Mountain!

_____
10 POINTS

(Look straight out.)

SPECIAL HINT: The first long mountain you see in front of you is **Massanutten Mountain**. It really *is* about 40 miles long! The **"V"- shaped opening** in the mountain is called **New Market Gap** and leads down west into the town of New Market and connects the road to the east with Luray. A **Civil War battle** took place at the New Market Gap in **1864**. Confederate General Breckinridge needed more troops so he brought along young student cadets from the Virginia Military Institute, hoping he wouldn't have to use them in the fight. Unfortunately, he needed them. Six of the 10 young cadets who died in that battle are buried on the grounds of **Virginia Military Institute** (VMI).

19
Find a Bird that Flies 200 MPH!

(Look---up in the sky.)

SPECIAL HINT: This bird is amazing! **Peregrine falcons** can dive at about **200 miles per hour!** They hit their prey (other birds), stun them, and grab them in mid-air as they fall toward the ground! Now that's *really fast food!*

NA

They build their nests on cliffs and pinnacles. A peregrine has a white belly and it looks like it is wearing a black "helmet" on its head. Some folks think it looks like it has dark sideburns. It is rare to see one . . . but then again, it is rare to stand on a forehead on top of a mountain! Good Luck!

full evergreen tree in front of our room—although few here

20

Find the Hitchin Posts that Point Which Way You Should Go!

10 POINTS

(As you leave the peak and head back down the trail--- on the left)

SPECIAL HINT: There are many trails at this intersection. It could be confusing, but simply follow the direction that the hitching post is pointing toward.

10 POINTS

21

Conduct a Painful Scientific Experiment!

(Count 45 steps past marker #18---look around---on the left of the trail.)

SPECIAL HINT: Find an **evergreen tree** on the left and touch the points of the needles several times with the end of one of your fingers. If it *doesn't* hurt it is a **Balsam fir** tree. If you say, "Ouch!"— you have discovered a **red spruce**! Which did you find? Both of these trees are **more commonly found in colder climates** like in Canada. At one time the climate *here* was much colder and there were many Balsam fir and red spruce trees in this "neck of the woods." When the climate got warmer they could no longer survive except in the highest elevations like on Stony Man Mountain!

REMEMBER . . . DON'T EVER PICK OR HARM ANY TREE OR PLANT. THEY ARE PROTECTED BY FEDERAL LAW.

10 POINTS

NOW . . .

FOLLOW THE BLUE BLAZES BACK TO THE TRAILHEAD.

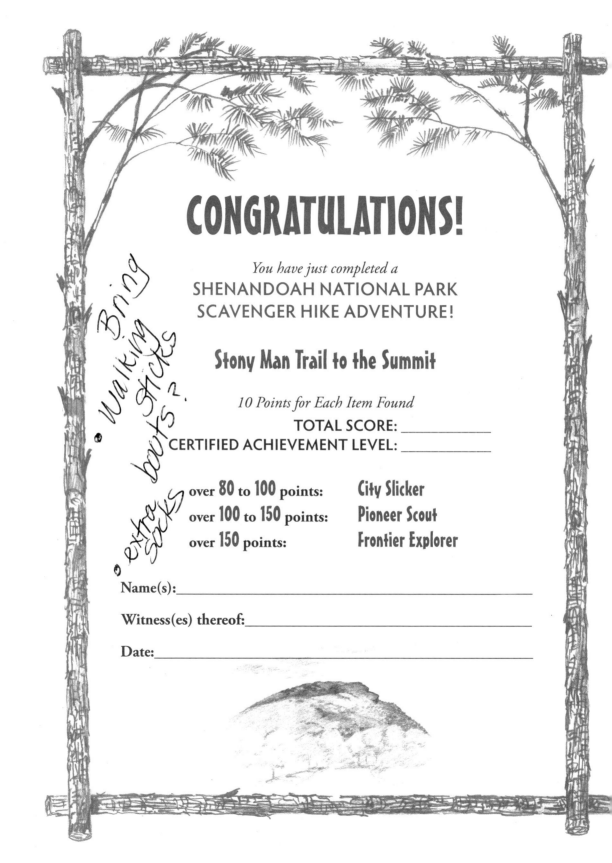

CONGRATULATIONS!

You have just completed a
SHENANDOAH NATIONAL PARK
SCAVENGER HIKE ADVENTURE!

Stony Man Trail to the Summit

10 Points for Each Item Found

TOTAL SCORE: _____

CERTIFIED ACHIEVEMENT LEVEL: _____

over **80** to **100** points: **City Slicker**
over **100** to **150** points: **Pioneer Scout**
over **150** points: **Frontier Explorer**

Name(s):_____

Witness(es) thereof:_____

Date:_____

Bring
Walking sticks?
• boots?
• extra socks

2 Mill Prong Trail to President Hoover's Hidden Cabin and Rapidan Camp

Scavenger Hike Adventure

MODERATE

3.6 MILES ROUNDTRIP

3-4 HOURS

Why This is a Great Trail! This unusual and unique Scavenger Hike Adventure leads to the former hidden **presidential retreat and cabin** once owned by **President Herbert Hoover!** You will rock-hop across 3 beautiful streams and find the **hypnotic waterfall** where the **president's wife, Lou Henry Hoover, would bring her guests for tea parties**! You will find a **drinking fountain** that archeologists learned really *isn't* a drinking fountain, a recently discovered **man-made trout pond**, the actual restored **cabin of the world's first person to appear on television,** and a **tree left to grow through the porch and roof** of President Hoover's cabin! **Vice-President Al Gore, President Jimmy Carter, President Franklin Roosevelt,** and President Hoover's good friend, **Charles Lindbergh**, all spent some time enjoying "Rapidan Camp." **Now it's your turn!**

Where's the Trail? The trailhead is located across the Skyline Drive from the Milam Gap parking area at **mile 52.8** in the Central District of the park. At the end of the parking lot there is a **painted crosswalk to guide you across the Skyline Drive.** You will hike on the Appalachian Trail for just a *few seconds* before coming to the intersection for Mill Prong Trail on the left.

About the Trail: This is a **MODERATE** trail that is a very pleasant combination of level and downhill all the way to Rapidan Camp. The mainly soft dirt trail leads down through an old apple orchard and is shaded the entire way. You will cross 3 streams using rocks as steps. Spring rains could mean wet socks (pack an extra pair). Returning is a combination of level and "uphill," but the level areas really break up the distance and this Scavenger Hike Adventure is **do-able for families with children at least 42 inches or so tall** . . . about the same requirement as riding a roller coaster.

How Long is This Hike? This Scavenger Hike Adventure is **3.6 miles roundtrip**. You should **allow 3-4 hours** so you can spend time exploring the incredible national treasures of Rapidan Camp!

Things To Hunt For
(Earn 10 points for each treasure you find.)

❶ Find the Left Turn that Doesn't Lead to Georgia!

10 POINTS

(First . . . cross Skyline Drive near the Trailhead sign---find the Mill Prong Trail marker---just after crossing the Skyline Drive.) SPECIAL HINT: At this intersection the **Appalachian Trail** continues south on to Georgia! You will need to turn left and head down **Mill Prong Trail** unless you have a strong interest in hiking to Georgia for a peach. Peaches . . . straight. . . **President Hoover's cabin . . . left!**

❷ Find the Fields of Ferns!

10 POINTS

(On both sides of the trail) SPECIAL HINT: As you begin the hike you are walking through an old apple orchard. In fact, **"Milam" apples** were once famous throughout the East. (You are at Milam Gap.) There are about 60 different kinds of ferns growing in the park. Cinnamon ferns, interrupted ferns, and hay-scented ferns are 3 of the many ferns that make Shenandoah National Park their home. Hey!!! Enjoy the beautiful ferns along this trail! PLEASE REMEMBER TO NEVER PICK OR HARM ANY PLANT IN SHENANDOAH NATIONAL PARK.

❸

Find the Giant Dead Holey Hemlock Tree with 2 Trunks!

_____
10 POINTS

(Hike for quite a while--- on the left of the trail---on the trail---you can't miss it---it is still standing.)

SPECIAL HINT: There are lots of **woodpecker holes** in this dead old **hemlock** tree that has too many branches to count! Notice the thick rough bark on this awesome tree! **President Hoover loved the beautiful hemlock trees** because the wonderful-smelling lacey branches of hemlock needles provided so much cool shade by his camp. Air conditioners had not been invented yet and giant hemlock trees really helped cool things down. A tiny bug from Asia, the **hemlock woolly adelgid (a-DELL-jid)**, has recently **killed most of the hemlock trees** in these mountains.

❹

Find & Walk Through the Fallen Dead Hemlock Tree!

_____
10 POINTS

(At a narrow opening---in the trunk)

SPECIAL HINT: The trail crew cut a narrow opening in the fallen trunk here for _you_ so you don't have to climb over it. The **Hoovers tried to avoid cutting down trees** when they built Rapidan Camp. They even built roofs _around_ trees rather than cut them down! You'll see!

❺

Find a Baker's Dozen of Rocks that will Lead you Across the Stream!

_____
10 POINTS

(About 13 rocks crossing the stream)

SPECIAL HINT: You will follow **Mill Prong** stream all along the way! It connects to the **Rapidan River** just a few steps behind President Hoover's cabin. He lived in the **"White House"** in Washington, D.C., and the **"Brown House"** at Rapidan Camp.

CAUTION: BE CAREFUL! WET ROCKS CAN BE AS SLIPPERY AS ICE.

6 Find 2 Boulders as Big as Whales!

(One on the left and one on the right of the trail---across from each other---a bit into the woods)
SPECIAL HINT: You can't miss these humongous boulders! At President Hoover's cabin the chimney was built around a giant boulder. Check it out when you get there!

10 POINTS

7 Find the Giant Tree with Giant Holes Pecked by the Second Largest Woodpecker in North America!

(20 feet off the trail---on the left side of the trail---you can't miss it)
SPECIAL HINT: The **pileated (pronounced Pile-ee-ated or Pill-ee-ated) woodpecker** sometimes makes holes big enough to stick your fist inside. This woodpecker is about as big as a crow. They often build their nests in the large oval-shaped holes. The pileated woodpecker is **black with a bright red crest** (top of its head). It is also white under its wings. When it is pecking away, it sounds like a **drumroll**! Listen for a drumroll in the woods!

10 POINTS

PLEASE ALWAYS STAY ON THE TRAIL!

8 Find the Perfect Tree for Baking a Cherry Pie!

(Count 8 steps after crossing the stream---on the right of the trail.)
SPECIAL HINT: This tree has **bark that looks like shredded paper!** The **yellow birch** wood burns at the perfect temperature to bake pies. Pioneers could control woodstove temperatures by using different combinations of wood. Early stoves didn't have a temperature dial. "John-boy, please turn up the oven one birch log."

NOTE: THE HORSE TRAIL TO RAPIDAN CAMP JOINS UP WITH THE MILL PRONG TRAIL JUST PAST THE YELLOW BIRCH TREE. FOLLOW THE PAINTED YELLOW BLAZES

ON THE TREES AND HIKE DOWN THE HILL. THE YELLOW BLAZES MEAN THIS IS A TRAIL FOR HORSES BUT PEOPLE ARE WELCOME, TOO.

10 POINTS

9

Find the "Fish For Fun" Stream!

(On the right---read all about it.)
SPECIAL HINT: This stream is **"catch and release."** A fisherman with a Virginia fishing license can catch a fish, but must return it to the stream and not harm it. **President Hoover loved fishing** and that is why he had his cabin built right next to the **Rapidan River**. PLEASE FOLLOW THE PARK'S FISHING RULES!

10 POINTS

10

Find Where the First Lady Took Guests for Tea!

(Hike a while---up ahead---go downhill--- on the right of the trail.)
SPECIAL HINT: This **waterfall** is named **Big Rock Falls . . .** you can guess why! The President's wife, **Lou Henry Hoover, loved to bring guests here for tea and snacks!** The first lady enjoyed horseback riding and nature. She was also the president of the **Girl Scouts of America.** Imagine her riding up here with a group of girl scouts or wives of dignitaries enjoying this beautiful waterfall!

Put your book away for now and enjoy the hike along beautiful Mill Prong stream.

President Hoover loved the sound of rushing water and that was another important reason he built Rapidan Camp just ahead.

10 POINTS

NEXT STOP: RAPIDAN CAMP! IN CASE ANYONE IS WONDERING . . . YOU ARE ALMOST THERE!
TAKE YOUR BOOK BACK OUT WHEN YOU ARRIVE AT RAPIDAN CAMP!

⑪ Find Rapidan Camp!

(Hike a while---to the "T" in the trail.)
SPECIAL HINT: You have entered the grounds of **Rapidan Camp!** There were once **13 buildings** here instead of just the 3 that you will see today. The local folks were elated that President Hoover chose to build his "summer White House" right here in their county. On August 17, 1929, they invited him to a special welcome celebration called **"Hoover Day"** at the **Madison County fairgrounds**. Locals were shocked when he *actually* accepted the invitation! They served **50 washtubs (15 gallons each) of "squirrel stew"** in tin cups to thousands of people. As the day went on they ran out of stew! Thank goodness they had also prepared 300 loaves of bread and 500 chickens! Planners were worried they might run out of food so each local family was asked to bring a picnic basket for the guest table. **Virginia's Governor Harry F. Byrd** flew in for the celebration in a blimp! That was some party! Welcome to Rapidan Camp!

10 POINTS

⑫ Find the Creel Cabin!

(At the "T" veer to the right---go down the steps---then count 20 steps---look on the left.)
SPECIAL HINT: This cabin was used by President Hoover's personal physician, **Dr. Boone**, and his chief of security and former F.B.I agent, **Mr. Richey.** Look carefully and find the tree that used to grow right through the roof!

There are 21 windows in this small cabin. Every summer volunteers move into **Creel** to help with tours and watch over the camp. What a great job to have!

10 POINTS

⓭

Find the Drinking Fountain that Really Isn't a Drinking Fountain!

---

10 POINTS

(Count 27 steps past the mess hall sign---take the side trail to the right.)

SPECIAL HINT: For many years everyone thought this was a **drinking fountain**. Archaeologists dug around the alleged drinking fountain and discovered it wasn't a drinking fountain after all! Instead, they found 7 little pools at the base and learned that this was a *decorative* **fountain.** Water spilled over 4 levels into the little pools.

⓮

Find the Camp Map!

---

10 POINTS

(Continue past the former "drinking fountain" to find the big map.)

SPECIAL HINT: The map shows the layout of all of the original **13 buildings** that used to be here! **President Hoover loved fishing** and sometimes he wouldn't even take time to change out of his suit and tie after arriving from the White House! He chose to build his summer White House here because it was within 100 miles of Washington, D.C., and was cooled by shade trees. Most important, it was on the beautiful Rapidan River and had great fishing!

⓯

Find the Ladder that Points to the Prime Minister's Cabin!

---

10 POINTS

(Follow the direction of the ladder--to the right.)

SPECIAL HINT: When volunteers are on site you can go inside the **Prime Minister's Cabin** and view interesting displays. Lou Henry Hoover's humorous list of **camp rules** is on a table as you enter the cabin. **Prime Minister Ramsay MacDonald** of Great Britain visited here with his daughter to meet President Hoover and discuss big issues after World War I. He and President Hoover sat together on a log and discussed how to secure freedom from war for future generations.

16

Find the Cabin of the World's First TV Star!

10 POINTS

(As you leave the Prime Minister's Cabin---take a right past the ladder---to the next cabin.)

SPECIAL HINT: When **President Hoover** was **Secretary of Commerce**, he gave a short speech that was broadcast on a new contraption called a **"television."** He was the **first person ever shown on TV!** In 1927 during this TV demonstration, he said, **"I am glad to welcome television as the latest product of scientific discovery."** The broadcast went to Washington, D.C., and he could have said, "Live from New York" (where he was).

If park volunteers are on hand, you might get lucky and be able to go inside President Hoover's cabin. You are always welcome to peek inside the windows.

17

Find the Tree that Grew Right Through the Roof and the Chimney that was Built Around a Boulder!

10 POINTS

(At President Hoover's cabin)
SPECIAL HINT: The Hoovers liked to leave Rapidan Camp as natural as possible! Just look around and you will see!

18

Find the Reason the Grocery List Didn't Match Up With the Camp's Menu!

10 POINTS

(Across the path from the cabin---small pool of water---on the right)
SPECIAL HINT: This small **fish pond** was custom-made for President Hoover. Beef hearts were always ordered on the grocery list, but never appeared on a dinner menu. Why? President Hoover was feeding them to the fish in this little pond.

⑲

Find the Exact Spot Where President Hoover Slept!

(Follow the back deck around the corner---go up two steps--stand on the landing.)
SPECIAL HINT: Peek inside the window and you'll see where President Hoover slept. His wife slept in the room next door so that she wasn't disturbed when phone calls and urgent messages were delivered throughout the night. In **1932**, when the nation's economy was having big troubles, **President Hoover was receiving about 150 phone calls at all times of the day and night!**

10 POINTS

⑳

Find the Fireplace that is Perfect for a Great Kodak Moment!

(In front of the "Brown House"---to the right)
SPECIAL HINT: This chimney/fireplace was used primarily as a spot to take **photographs** of the president with his guests. President Hoover was an **incredible humanitarian** and gave so much for others throughout the world! After World War II he was asked to help coordinate feeding the hungry in Europe as he had done after World War I. President Hoover and his wife, Lou, also **built a school** for the children who lived in this area and provided a teacher to teach both the children and their parents. *"Smile" as you capture the moment at this historical chimney!*

It is a special privilege to visit this national historic landmark and experience the same joy and tranquility of nature that President Herbert Hoover and the First Lady loved so much!

10 POINTS

NOW ... HEAD ON PAST THE OUTDOOR FIREPLACE. BE SURE TO CHECK THE TRAIL SIGNS AND RETURN TO MILAM GAP AND GO NORTH ON THE AT

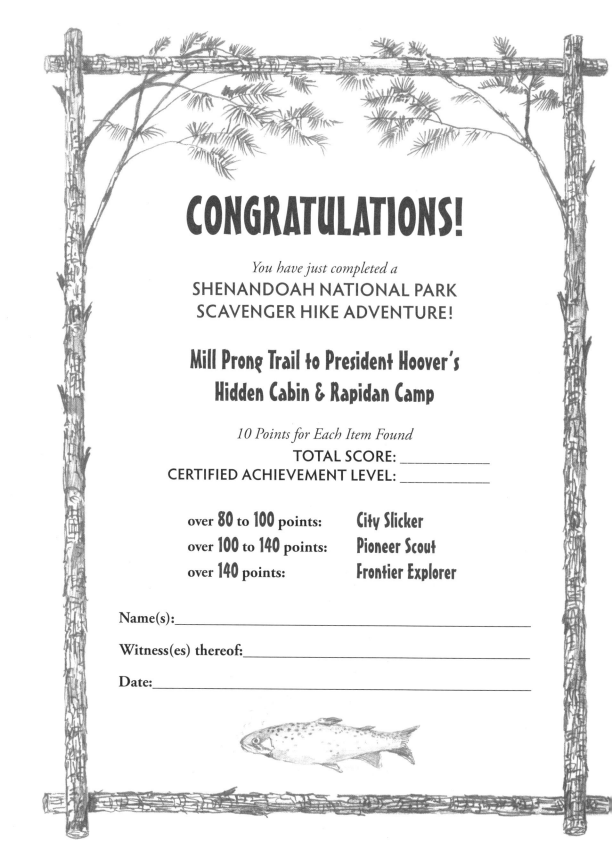

CONGRATULATIONS!

You have just completed a
SHENANDOAH NATIONAL PARK
SCAVENGER HIKE ADVENTURE!

Mill Prong Trail to President Hoover's Hidden Cabin & Rapidan Camp

10 Points for Each Item Found
TOTAL SCORE: _____
CERTIFIED ACHIEVEMENT LEVEL: _____

over **80** to **100** points: **City Slicker**
over **100** to **140** points: **Pioneer Scout**
over **140** points: **Frontier Explorer**

Name(s):_____

Witness(es) thereof:_____

Date:_____

The Limberlost Trail

Why This is a Great Trail! This Scavenger Hike Adventure is absolutely amazing! You will see with your very own eyes an **"Extreme Makeover" in progress!** Nature is hard at work *re-creating* this very special place after **hurricanes, bugs, people, and ice storms** took down tree after tree over the last 100 years. You will find thousands of *fallen dead trees* scattered all over the forest like **giant pick-up sticks** and thousands of *brand new trees and plants* popping up everywhere! You will find **many new "residents"** and 1 critter that can hold over 1,100 grass seeds in its mouth! Find a new grove of **trees that smell just like root beer!** Find a **tree that was clawed by a very large bear**, rocks that look like **giant green teeth,** and a **mysterious log structure!** You will walk on a boardwalk and find **old apple trees from long ago** when a settler had an orchard here. **Caution: This trail is undergoing an Extreme Makeover!** Nature is busy painting a new landscape and it will be a masterpiece!!!

Where's the Trail? The trailhead is at **milepost 43** on the east side of Skyline Drive in the Central District of the park. There is a large sign for the Limberlost Trail and plenty of paved parking near the trailhead.

About the Trail: This trail is an **EASY** level loop. It is made of crushed greenstone and is *wheelchair-and-stroller-navigable.* There are many benches along the way to sit and watch nature's *Extreme Makeover* in progress. This forest and trail is believed to have been named after a popular novel from the early 1900s, *The Girl of the Limberlost.* It is the story of a young girl who finds peace and comfort in a swampy forest in Indiana named the Limberlost.

How Long is This Hike? This Scavenger Hike Adventure is a **1.3-mile loop** and will take explorers **a bit less than an hour.**

Things To Hunt For

(Earn 10 points for each treasure you find.)

❶ Find the Black Lava/Volcano Rock Disguised in Green!

(10 steps past the large trail sign---on the right)

SPECIAL HINT: This boulder used to be a totally **black lava /volcano rock** before it sat on the bottom of the ocean that once covered the Limberlost. **Heat and pressure** under the ocean **changed it into** the most common rock in Shenandoah National Park . . . **greenstone.** Look closely and you can still see where **white quartz** filled up some of the holes made by hot gases bubbling out of the lava rock as it cooled. After all of that commotion, this boulder deserves a peaceful rest. It **started its journey about 600 million years ago** and ended up right here on this trail! How was *your* trip here?

10 POINTS

❷ Find the Giant Welcome Mat for Horses!

(At the intersection with the horse trail)

SPECIAL HINT: Stand on the rubber mat and look to the right for the **yellow blaze** on the tree. The yellow rectangle (blaze) shows that a **horse trail** is crossing through the Limberlost. The mat helps protect Limberlost Trail from the horses' hooves. About 20 horses live up the trail a piece by Skyland Resort. If you go visit them, please say "Hello" to Paint, Ginger, and Molly. Giddy-up!

10 POINTS

❸ Find a Star-Shaped Tree Stump!

(Just past the bench---on the left of the trail)

SPECIAL HINT: This hemlock tree stump has been cut almost level with the ground. Hundreds of beautiful giant **hemlock trees** once lived here in the Limberlost. Visitors staying at

Skyland Resort about 100 years ago, before Shenandoah National Park even existed, would come to the Limberlost on horseback just to have a picnic under the cool shade of these awesome trees. A tiny insect from Asia, the **hemlock woolly adelgid (pronounced a-DEL-jid)**, killed almost all of the hemlocks in Shenandoah National Park. Nature took one look at the thousands of fallen trees and said, "It's time for an **Extreme Makeover**"!

10 POINTS

④ Find the Mountain Laurel Tunnel!

Count 89 steps past the same bench in clue #3---on both sides of the trail.)
SPECIAL HINT: **Mountain laurel** can live in the shade, but it also enjoys the new sunshine here at Limberlost! It is a large shrub or small tree and has thick **evergreen leaves about as long as your finger.** Touch a leaf . . . it feels like **leather**! When the mountain laurel is blooming here, it is like walking through a **spectacular pink-and-white bouquet of flowers**!

REMEMBER TO NEVER PICK OR HARM A PLANT HERE IN THE PARK!

10 POINTS

⑤ Find a Critter that Can Hold 1,169 Grass Seeds in its Mouth!

(All along the trail---go on to #6 as you look.)
SPECIAL HINT: **Chipmunks** live all around you! Many of them have just recently moved here to the Limberlost. You can see the **Extreme Makeover** in progress all around you! New plants, shrubs, and grasses are sprouting up everywhere. Chipmunks love the seeds and berries and it's just like a brand new **"restaurant"** for those cute little critters! Chipmunks scurry about and gather and hide seeds in and under the fallen trees. A scientist once found a chipmunk with **1,169 grass seeds** in its cheek pouches!

10 POINTS

6

Find the Giant Fungus Among Us!

10 POINTS

(Look behind the bench on the left of the trail---and across the trail from the bench--- to the right--- on the trees.)
SPECIAL HINT: The large strange looking bumps on the trees are actually a **fungus**. It is just another interesting and natural part of nature. It is a native "fungus among us." It won't kill the tree unless it grows completely around the trunk.

7

Find the Old Rag Fire Road!

10 POINTS

(Up ahead)
SPECIAL HINT: Fire roads are cut into the mountains so firefighters have a way to quickly reach a fire. Some **fire roads** were once **old pioneer roads**. You will cross the Old Rag fire road and continue on the trail. **Old Rag** is the name of a popular *"ragged"* and really rocky mountain. It is also a very *"old"* mountain, so now you know how "Old Rag" got its name!

8

Find the Root Beer Stand!

10 POINTS

(Along both sides of the trail after you cross the fire road)
SPECIAL HINT: Find the **young trees that all look alike**. *Carefully and lightly* scratch a twig with your fingernail. You will smell root beer! Mmmmmm . . . this tree smells great! A group of trees is called a **"stand."** Hey! I guess you could say you found a **root beer stand!** In fact, root beer is sometimes called *"birch beer."* This stand of **black birch** trees is already rapidly spreading in the **Extreme Makeover** of the Limberlost. Someday these trees might grow to 75 feet tall!

NEVER PICK ANY PLANT OR FLOWER IN THE NATIONAL PARK. ALL PLANTS AND ANIMALS ARE PROTECTED BY FEDERAL LAW.

9

Find 2 Fallen Giants!

(Before the next bench---on the right and left of the trail)
SPECIAL HINT: These giant **hemlock tree stumps** are hundreds of years old! If you are quite curious and want to take a l---o---n---g break, sit

on a stump and count each tiny little ring! Each ring is one year of tree growth. Many of the beautiful **hemlock trees** in the park **were 300-400 years old. Addie Nairn Pollock** had **Massanutten Lodge** built at Skyland Resort in 1911 as **her summer retreat.** She loved these hemlock trees and personally bought 100 of them here in Limberlost so a logging company would not cut them down. **She paid $10 for each tree.**

10 POINTS

⑩

Find the Rock Formation that Looks Like Giant Greenish Teeth!

(On the left side of the trail---at the intersection with Whiteoak Canyon Trail)
SPECIAL HINT: This unusual group of boulders was created when **lava flowed** like a giant deep river over this area and **as it slowly cooled it created this formation.** If you look at the top of the boulders you will find that many of the individual sections have 5 sides. When mud dries in a mud puddle it will also crack in the very same kind of 5-sided design. Hmmmm. Very interesting! If this was a science book we would tell you that you might see other formations like this throughout the park and it is called **"columnar jointing."** Since this is not a science book . . . forget we said that!

10 POINTS

⑪

Find the Fabulous Ferns in the Forest!

(Sit on the next bench---push your chin 3 inches to the left---look straight across the trail.)
SPECIAL HINT: There are over **60 different kinds of ferns** in Shenandoah National Park. This is one of them and it is called an **"interrupted fern."**   Take a moment and examine the intricate delicate beauty and design of these fabulous ferns. Ahhhhh . . . please don't interrupt your fellow hikers as they also discover these *"interrupted ferns."* Remember . . . leave everything in the park for others to see.

NEVER TAKE OR PICK ANYTHING IN THIS AWESOME NATIONAL PARK.

10 POINTS

⑫

Find the Tiny Log Structure!

_____

10 POINTS

(Cross the bridge---hike a bit---then count 17 steps from the sharp right hand turn in the trail---look around to the right.) SPECIAL HINT: This miniature log cabin was once inhabited by a family of tiny elves who migrated here centuries ago from Denmark. The elves played many musical instruments and late at night the **Limberlost** air was filled with Danish music and the sweet smell of cheese danishes! Either that . . . or this log enclosure surrounds a **measuring tool that monitors the water table.**

⑬

Find the Awesome Oak Tree that Explains Why Some Cuckoo Birds Like To Visit Shenandoah National Park Each Year!

(Behind the next bench---on the right) SPECIAL HINT: **This old oak tree has a story to tell. Listen to what this tree has to say:**

"About 30 years ago **gypsy moth caterpillars** were brought to the United States to breed with **silkworms** to make more silk. That never worked. What is worse, those caterpillars escaped and came here and ate oak tree leaves. They **killed a lot of the oak trees**, but it is all under better control now. There are still thousands of oak trees in the park just like me. As luck would have it, **cuckoo birds** absolutely love to snack on gypsy moth caterpillars.

Black billed
Brown on top
white under
Red eye ring
black decurved bill
long tail faint white spots
song repitition

Somehow they heard about the caterpillars being here and so now some cuckoo birds visit here for a few weeks each year to enjoy eating them. This all sounds kind of cuckoo, but it is really a true story. And that is all I have to say about that."

10 POINTS

⑭

Find a White-Tailed Deer!

(Go on to #15 as you look all along the trail and in the forest.)
SPECIAL HINT: **White-tailed deer** like to eat leaves from oak trees, and they also enjoy grasses, apples, blackberries, raspberries, blueberries, and acorns. When a white-tailed deer senses danger its **tail** will go up like **a white flag** to warn other deer!

IF YOU ALREADY SAW A WHITE-TAILED DEER ON THIS TRAIL . . . GIVE YOURSELF THE POINTS!

10 POINTS

⑮

Find the Apple Orchard!

(Count 40 steps past the boardwalk---look on the right of the trail.)
SPECIAL HINT: You are walking through an old **apple orchard** that was once part of a pioneer's farm. **Many people lived in this area** before the land was made into a national park. For so many mountain folks it was a *very sad* day when **they were forced to move.** At that time this land was part of a farm and cows probably napped under these apple trees. Now, it's time to *mooove* along.

10 POINTS

16

Find Bear Claw Marks Made by a Very Large Bear!

10 POINTS

(Count 36 steps past the next bench---look around on the left---close to the trail---on a tree.)

SPECIAL HINT: The **black bear** stood up on its hind legs to claw this tree. **When it was born** it was only about the **size of a can of soda** and was **bald and toothless . . .** but already **had claws!** A black bear's claws may be 2 inches long, and the padding on the bottom of its paws helps it walk very quietly through the forest.

NEVER RUN FROM OR TURN YOUR BACK ON A BEAR. REVIEW THE GUIDELINES ON BEARS IN THE FRONT OF THE BOOK.

17

Find Spoonwood!

10 POINTS

(Straight ahead---you can't possibly miss it---on both sides of the trail---as you near the end of the trail)

SPECIAL HINT: Pioneers used the wood from mountain laurel to make spoons! **Mountain laurel has short, thick, leathery leaves.** This is like a *jungle* of mountain laurel!

CONGRATULATIONS!

You have just completed a
SHENANDOAH NATIONAL PARK
SCAVENGER HIKE ADVENTURE!

Limberlost Trail

10 Points for Each Item Found

TOTAL SCORE: _____

CERTIFIED ACHIEVEMENT LEVEL: _____

over **50** to **90** points:	**City Slicker**
over **90** to **130** points:	**Pioneer Scout**
over **130** points:	**Frontier Explorer**

Name(s):_____

Witness(es) thereof:_____

Date:_____

4

Scavenger Hike Adventure

MODERATE

2.8 MILE LOOP

3 HOURS

Hawksbill Summit Via the Appalachian Trail and Salamander Trail

Why This is a Great Trail! This is a very special Scavenger Hike Adventure! It leads to **Hawksbill Summit**, the **highest peak** in the entire Shenandoah National Park (**about 4,050 feet elevation)!** You will find **breathtaking views of the mountains and the valley** thousands of feet below as you hike along the ridge and a spectacular **360-degree view at the top!** You will find 3 unusual mountainsides of **broken rocks called "talus"** and beautiful **purple flowering raspberries** in May through September. On the peak of Hawksbill Mountain you will find **2 metal compasses** embedded in concrete, **miniature oak trees,** and you may find **a bird that flies up to 200 miles per hour** as it catches its prey in mid-air!!! This Scavenger Hike Adventure will definitely be the high point of your visit to this magnificent national park!

Where's the Trail? The trailhead is located on the west side of Skyline Drive at **mile 45.6** in the Central District of the park. There is a sign that says "Hawksbill Gap." **Important note: There are 2 trail routes to the summit at this parking area. One of the trail entrances has a really nice sign, 3 boulders at the entry point, and it looks just so inviting. NO! NO! NO!** That trail route is like hiking almost a mile up an escalator that is not moving! **At the north end of the parking lot is the Appalachian Trail.** That is your ticket to the top. **Take the AT!**

About the Trail: This is a **MODERATE** loop trail. It is a bit uphill at first, but not really very hard. You'll probably find it more difficult hiking *down* the short steep route back to your car. The hike begins on the Appalachian Trail and for a mile provides a great AT adventure! You will then take Salamander Trail up to the peak. It is rocky in some sections and you should definitely leave your sandals and flip-flops at home for this one! After reaching the summit, take the short and steep Lower Hawksbill Trail to complete the loop back to your car.

How Long is This Hike? This Scavenger Hike Adventure is a 2.8-mile loop. You should allow 3 hours so you can spend time enjoying the incredible views at the top!

Things To Hunt For
(Earn 10 points for each treasure you find.)

❶

Find the 2,175-Mile-Long Appalachian Trail!

_____
10 POINTS

(Go to the north end of the parking lot---about 50 yards into the woods---to the AT intersection.)

SPECIAL HINT: Go left at the "T." The **Appalachian Trail** is over 70 years old and took 15 years to build. There is a sign at Springer Mountain, Georgia (the southern starting point), that describes the AT as **"A footpath for those who seek fellowship with the wilderness."** Welcome to the world-famous Appalachian Trail!

❷

Find the Landing Zone for Flying Squirrels!

_____
10 POINTS

(Count 72 steps from the AT sign---find a boulder on the right side of the trail.)
SPECIAL HINT: Find the **large boulder next to a smaller boulder** that has a striped maple tree growing out of it. The bigger boulder looks like it is covered with **brown dead leaves,** but it is really a **lichen (pronounced LIKE-in)** and is called **rock tripe**. The rock tripe is a combination of **algae and fungus** and is a favorite snack of **flying squirrels!** You will see many more "landing zones" along this trail.

❸ Find a Special Tree Used by Indians!

10 POINTS

(Count 14 steps past the boulder with lichen in #2---the tree is on the left---close to the trail.)

SPECIAL HINT: This **yellow birch** tree has 2 trunks and has **yellowish-silverish shiny bark** that in some places looks like **shredded paper!** It also has horizontal lines on the trunk. What is cool about this unusual tree is that there is **oil in the bark** so **pioneers and Indians** could use it to **start fires even when the bark was wet.** This tree was probably really appreciated by *hungry, cold* Indians and pioneers on *chilly wet* days! It is tough to make squirrel stew without a fire.

❹ Find the Tree With 2 White Blazes (Rectangles)!

10 POINTS

(On the left side of the trail)

SPECIAL HINT: Two white rectangles (blazes) painted on a tree means that the **AT is changing direction.** Remember, **thru-hikers** are traveling on this trail for the **entire 2,175 miles** and so these markers are especially important for them. Volunteers paint the blazes and hikers should always be able to see the next white blaze up the trail.

❺ Find the Boulder that Looks Like the Head of a Dinosaur!

(On the right side of the trail---just 3 steps off the trail---where there are 2 boulders that are lying flat on the ground)

SPECIAL HINT: The boulder closest to the trail is about the same actual size and shape of the head of a **tyrannosaurus rex** dinosaur. It looks as if the T-Rex is looking up the hill. This boulder is called "**greenstone**" and if it was broken in half you would see very dark green coloring inside. Greenstone boulders gradually weather and fade on the outside from dark green to gray. Greenstone is the **most common kind of rock** found in Shenandoah National Park. By the way, fossil footprints of real dinosaurs have been found in **Culpeper, Virginia** . . . just east of the national park.

6 Find the Awesome Fungus Among Us!

(Count 17 steps past the T-Rex---on the broken-off tree---on the right side of the trail.)
SPECIAL HINT: This tree was snapped off at the top by very high winds. **Give yourself the points for just finding the tree!** Look for **the awesome fungus** growing on this tree! The fungus is in **four layers** with dark brown at the top, light brown next, off-white in the middle, and brownish-orange at the bottom. **Does it look like a chocolate marshmallow cookie to you?** Use your imagination! This fungus will help break down the stump of this tree and will put nutrients and minerals back into the soil.

DO NOT EAT THIS FUNGUS!

10 POINTS

7 Find a Boulder that Needs a Toothbrush!

(On the left of the trail---as you go up the hill)
SPECIAL HINT: The boulder is **bigger than an SUV** and looks like **a rock full of teeth** . . . lots of teeth! Lakes of red fiery **lava** once covered this area about **570 million years ago** . . . give or take a year or 2 . . . and cooled into these unusual shapes. This was once **black lava rock** before it changed to **greenstone**. You'll see similar formations throughout the national park because the lava lakes were humongous. The special **5-6-sided columns** that look like teeth are called "**dikes**."

10 POINTS

8

Find the Mountain of Broken Rocks!

(On the left)

SPECIAL HINT: Scientists say the **Blue Ridge Mountains** used to be as high as the Rocky Mountains (perhaps 3 times as high as they are today)! **Freezing and melting water** in cracks of boulders **helped break these rocks** into small pieces and they rolled off the top of the mountain. The mountains of broken rocks are called "**talus.**" Look up really high to see where some of the rocks came from. By the way, **rattlesnakes** like to live in talus slopes like these. It is their "home sweet home" or "rock sweet rock."

CAUTION: IF A RATTLESNAKE GETS FRIGHTENED, IT MAY TRY TO DEFEND ITS HOME. REMEMBER THAT YOU ARE THE "VISITOR" HERE. STAY ON THE TRAIL!

10 POINTS

9

Find Something that Looks Like Bright Yellow Spray Paint!

(On the broken rocks---on the left)

SPECIAL HINT: The bright yellow spots on the rocks are lichen. **Lichen (still pronounced LIKE-in)** is a combination of **algae** and **fungus** and comes in many shapes and colors. This one is often called **spray paint lichen.** What is really cool is that the algae's job is to use the sun and provide food for the fungus and the fungus' job is to hold on to the rock. They are a great team! Amazing!

ALL PLANTS AND LICHEN ARE PROTECTED IN SHENANDOAH NATIONAL PARK.
                    PLEASE BE CAREFUL NOT TO HARM THEM.

10 POINTS

10

Find a Purple Flowering Raspberry Plant!

_____
10 POINTS

(On both sides of the trail)
SPECIAL HINT: This **flowering raspberry plant** blooms from May throughout the summer and has **very large leaves shaped like a big maple tree leaf.** The beautiful flowers are rose and purple. It does grow a red berry that is edible, but it is tasteless. On this plant you can often find **berries and flowers at the same time.** What a plant!

11

Find the Salamander Trail that Leads to Hawksbill Peak!

_____
10 POINTS

(Hike a while---see the concrete marker at the trail junction.)
SPECIAL HINT: Turn left and hike on up **Salamander Trail**!

12

Find the Giant "Pick-Up Sticks"

_____
10 POINTS

(On both sides of the trail---after a sharp right turn)
SPECIAL HINT: **High winds, ice, landslides, hurricanes, snow, insects, and disease** constantly change the forest. The fallen trees all around you look like giant pick-up sticks! You can tell by the exposed tree roots that many of the fallen trees in this area were blown over by high winds.

13

Find a Salamander!

_____
10 POINTS

(Look down along both sides of the trail as you continue hiking.)
SPECIAL HINT: This is called Salamander Trail for a reason. Can you guess why? Please do not step off the trail or move any rocks or branches, to protect the "locals." Welcome to the very special neighborhood of the **Shenandoah Salamander**. It only lives in one place in the entire world . . . here in Shenandoah National Park! The red-backed salamander is very rare and special. Give yourself the points for finding any crawling critter and 10 bonus points if you catch a glimpse of a salamander. All of the 14 different kinds of salamanders living in the park have a special home. Please be careful. **Stay on the trail**.

endangered exclusively

⑭

Find the Good News Sign!

10 POINTS

(On the right side of the trail)
SPECIAL HINT: The sign says, "No camping beyond this point." The reason it is **"good news"** for you is that it also means **you are only 1/4-mile from a man-made structure.** Backcountry camping is not allowed anywhere near buildings and roads. You are very close to **Byrds Nest Shelter #2,** which is just a few seconds from the **summit of Hawksbill Mountain. You are almost there** . . . keep *"sala-meandering"* on up!

⑮

Find a Tunnel of Mountain Laurel!

blooms may–Jun

10 POINTS

(On both sides of the trail---looks like a tunnel)
SPECIAL HINT:
Mountain laurel has **short, leathery, evergreen leaves** about **as long as your finger** and blooms with a **pale pink or even purplish flower** in the spring. Mountain laurel blooms in large clusters and it is like walking inside a giant bouquet when they are in bloom in the spring. **Pioneers used the wood** from mountain laurel **to make spoons!**

⑯

Find Bear Scat!

(All along the trail---go on to #17 as you search.)
SPECIAL HINT: This area is like **a produce department for bears.** It is filled with blueberries, gooseberries, raspberries, and oak tree acorns. **Welcome to "Bearadise"!** This is a perfect place for a bear that is always "hungry as a bear"! Bears spend most of the day searching for something to eat. **Bear scat** (droppings) is usually **dark in color** and you can often guess what the bear has been eating by looking

very closely at the scat. ***Do not touch the scat with your fingers***. If you want to conduct a closer investigation of the scat . . . ***poke it with a stick.***

REMEMBER . . . NEVER RUN FROM A BEAR OR APPROACH A BEAR! NEVER TURN YOUR BACK ON A BEAR!

10 POINTS

⑰
Find Hawksbill Fire Road!

10 POINTS

(Look through the woods---on the right.)
SPECIAL HINT: Fire roads often follow old roads that were once used by mountain residents to get their farm crops or timber products to market. Today they are called **"fire roads"** and are used to get equipment and firefighters to forest fires. Hawksbill Fire Road goes all the way back down to Skyline Drive.

⑱
Find and Shake Hands with a Friendly Tree!

10 POINTS

(At the next overlook---count 8 steps farther on the trail---the tree is on the left.)
SPECIAL HINT: There is a very sharp right turn at this overlook point. Find the **Balsam fir** tree and introduce yourself with a handshake. The **needles** of a fir tree are **soft** and friendly, unlike the pointed sharp needles of the red spruce that also lives up here on this mountain. Both of these trees are usually found in much colder climates. **Glaciers pushed the seeds** down here during an Ice Age a very long time ago.

⑲
Find 4 Miniature Oak Trees!

10 POINTS

(Surrounding the next overlook---look around you.)
SPECIAL HINT: At this very high elevation **weather conditions are very harsh and extreme.** Trees adapt by staying closer to the ground where it is not as windy and not as cold. These mighty oak trees are many times taller at lower elevations. Size up these **"miniature"** oak trees. It is amazing!

20

Find the Byrds Nest!

10 POINTS

(Turn left onto the fire road.)
 SPECIAL HINT: **Senator Harry F. Byrd, Sr.,** of Virginia donated money to build 4 shelters in Shenandoah National Park. This shelter has a roof and 3 walls and is called **Byrds Nest #2.** Senator Byrd once had a private family cabin at Skyland Resort. It is still there and you could rent it for your vacation. Can you guess what it is called?

21

Find a Bird that Flies 200 M.P.H!

10 POINTS

(Look to the left while standing on the rocky cliff---in front of the Byrds Nest.)
SPECIAL HINT: **Peregrine Falcons** have been **re-introduced in Shenandoah National Park** after nearly becoming extinct. The falcons that used to live here ate birds that ate caterpillars that ate plants that farmers treated with a chemical called **DDT.** What a mess of events that was! DDT softened the shells of falcon eggs and killed the falcons. Look for white falcon droppings on the cliffs to the left. Rangers feed the falcons mice and an occasional fancy meal of Oklahoma quail. Hopes are that the chicks will return and will nest in their natural cliff homes in Shenandoah. It is too soon to tell if that is going to happen. They **dive** after their prey **at about 200 m.p.h.** and capture them in mid-air. Wow! **That's very fast food!**

22

Find 2 Metal Compasses Embedded in Concrete!

10 POINTS

(On the look-out platform)
SPECIAL HINT: It is awesome here! These views just might knock your hiking socks off! Be sure to put them back on before you head down the trail! There are actually **2 compasses** that point out cities and mountain peaks in the distance. Check it out!

23

Find the Right Trail To Get Back to Your Car!

10 POINTS

Go back down the fire road---go left on Lower Hawksbill Trail---check the concrete marker to be sure you're going the right way.)
SPECIAL HINT: Be sure to read the concrete marker so you are heading back on **Lower Hawksbill Trail** where your car is.

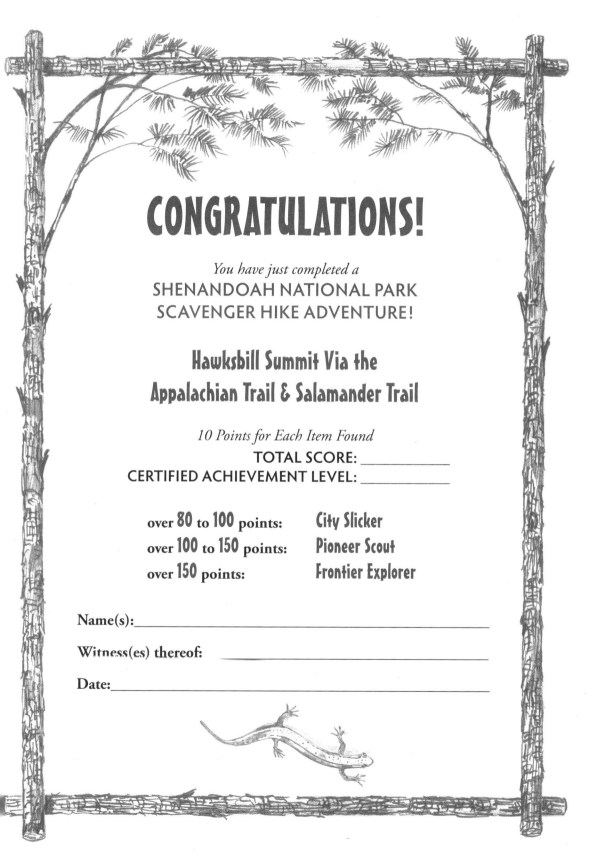

CONGRATULATIONS!

You have just completed a
SHENANDOAH NATIONAL PARK
SCAVENGER HIKE ADVENTURE!

Hawksbill Summit Via the
Appalachian Trail & Salamander Trail

10 Points for Each Item Found
TOTAL SCORE: _____
CERTIFIED ACHIEVEMENT LEVEL: _____

over **80** to **100** points: **City Slicker**
over **100** to **150** points: **Pioneer Scout**
over **150** points: **Frontier Explorer**

Name(s):_____

Witness(es) thereof: _____

Date:_____

Whiteoak Canyon Trail to the First Waterfall

Why This is a Great Trail! This Scavenger Hike Adventure leads to a very special place that could be your *absolutely, positively* **best picnic site ever!** Why??? This flat rock area overlooks an **awesome 86-foot-high waterfall**! You will peer through a *unique* **tree telescope** and discover a **plant used by pioneers to make spoons!** You will **scratch and sniff a tree** that will immediately make you thirsty and you will find over 20 large holes in one tree made by the **giant pileated woodpecker.** On this Scavenger Hike Adventure you will find a mysterious **forest of dead trees** as you hike into Whiteoak Canyon and the place where **huge swimming parties** were held in the late 1800s. Over 100 years ago groups hiked from the **Skyland Resort** as a marching band and the **resort owner/manager, George Freeman Pollock**, escorted them to this special waterfall! Today, the only music you will hear is the melody of the mountain stream as it leads you to this truly incredible waterfall!

Where's the Trail? The trailhead is located on the east side of the Skyline Drive at **mile 42.6** in the Central District of the park. There is a large parking lot for 40 cars located just across from the south entrance to the world-famous Skyland Resort.

About the Trail: This **MODERATE** Scavenger Hike Adventure leads down into Whiteoak Canyon on one of the most popular trails in Shenandoah National Park. A hiking stick would come in handy for support and balance in areas that might have slippery rocks. It is not very steep and is a great half-day adventure! Take plenty of water and snacks for a picnic. PB&J would taste awesome at the falls!

How Long is This Hike? This Scavenger Hike Adventure is **4.8 miles roundtrip** and will take your exploration team **about 4 hours** or so!

Things To Hunt For

(Earn 10 points for each treasure you find.)

❶

Find a Quadruplet Trunked White Oak Tree!

(Count 80 steps from the trailhead---on the right---close to the trail.)
SPECIAL HINT: This magnificent **white oak tree** has **4 trunks!**
Indians would crack open the acorns and put the inside part
(called acorn meat) in a basket. Then they would tie the basket
to a tree and put it in a fast-moving stream to strain out the bitter
flavor. They would use the acorn "meat"
to make **acorn bread**. Soooo . . . do you
want that sandwich on wheat or
acorn bread?

10 POINTS

❷

Find the Wall of Roots!

(After a fairly sharp right turn
in the trail---on the right-
--in a field of ferns)
SPECIAL HINT: These
2 trees crashed down to the
ground and now you can see
their roots. Shenandoah National Park
sometimes gets **hurricane winds** that blow trees down.

**CONTINUE TO FOLLOW THE BLUE BLAZES
(RECTANGLES) WHICH MEAN YOU ARE ON A FOOT
TRAIL.**

10 POINTS

❸

Find the Giant Tree Telescope and Look Through Its Lens!

(On the right---practically touching the trail---on a slight
downward slope)
SPECIAL HINT: Is this telescope awesome or what! Peer
through the hole in this totally cool telescope tree and find
mountain laurel. It has **short, thick, leathery leaves**. Mountain
laurel is an evergreen plant (stays green year-round). It is
beautiful when the pink-and-white flowers are blooming. The
leaves are **poisonous** to eat. Pioneers used the wood to make
spoons.

10 POINTS

4

Find Lots of Mountain Laurel!

10 POINTS

(On the left and right of the trail)
SPECIAL HINT: You won't need a telescope to find this! **Mountain laurel** is lining both sides of the trail. The gnarly, tangled trunks of mountain laurel sometimes grow so close together that pioneers could not even get through it. Pioneers called mountain laurel **"ivy."**

5

Find a Log Footbridge!

10 POINTS

(Up ahead)
SPECIAL HINT: Park trail crews often build log bridges so you can keep your feet dry. Dry feet . . . are happy feet!

6

Find Limberlost Trail!

10 POINTS

(The next path that crosses your trail)
SPECIAL HINT: The area you are entering is called *Limberlost*.
The name may have come from a popular novel published in 1909, *A Girl of the Limberlost.* The young girl in that novel lived in Indiana next to a swamp called Limberlost, where she went to escape from her difficult homelife. George F. Pollock's wife, **Addie Nairn Pollock**, loved this area and **bought 100** of the **large hemlock trees ($10 each**) that were once here **so that they wouldn't be cut down by loggers.**

7

Find 20 Holes (or more) in One Tree!

10 POINTS

(Count 34 steps past the Limberlost Trail intersection---on the right---on a tree---look up high.)
SPECIAL HINT: The **pileated woodpecker** is one of the largest woodpeckers in all of North America. Whoa! It pecks huge holes that are often in an oval shape. You can call this bird the **Pile-ee-ated** woodpecker or the **Pill-ee-ated** woodpecker. It doesn't mind which . . . it will answer to both!

❽
Find the Mysterious Forest of Dead Trees!

10 POINTS

(Cross the fire road---continue on the trail---look on both sides of the trail.)

SPECIAL HINT: Look for a forest with thousands of dead trees. **Gypsy moth caterpillars** and the **hemlock woolly adelgid (pronounced a-DEL-jid)** are 2 insects that wiped out many of these trees. Fortunately, each insect always seems to affect only 1 kind of tree. The caterpillars ate oak leaves and the hemlock woolly adelgid sucked the sap from the needles of the hemlock trees. New plants and trees will soon replace this "dead" forest. It won't take long!

❾
Find the Really, Really, NO Really Unusual Rock Formation!

10 POINTS

(On the left---at the next trail intersection)

SPECIAL HINT: OK, picture this! Deep lakes of **molten lava** covered this area. **As it cooled these rocks were formed.** If you look at the top of some of them you will notice they are like "columns" with **5 or more sides.** If you were a geologist you might say, "Goodness, what a fine example of *columnar jointing*!" You only have to say that if you are a geologist. Otherwise, you might just say "Wow!"

❿
Find a Tree and "Scratch & Sniff"!

10 POINTS

(Count 32 steps past the national park "backcountry" sign---look on the left and right of the trail.)

SPECIAL HINT: Carefully scratch a thin branch or stem of this young tree and take a deep whiff. The aroma will make you thirsty or at least remind you of a special drink . . . **root beer!** These **black birch** trees are replacing the hemlocks and oak trees that were killed by insects. By the way, since this is now backcountry, you can pitch your tent!

BE CAREFUL NOT TO PICK OR HARM ANY PLANT IN THE NATIONAL PARK. ALL PLANTS AND TREES AND FLOWERS ARE PROTECTED BY LAW.

⓫

Find an Awesome Round Tree Bench & Take a Break!

_____
10 POINTS

(On the right of the trail---at the bottom of a tree---where roots are traveling across the trail)
SPECIAL HINT: You might want to sit on this **awesome round tree bench** and rest your feet!

⓬

Find Whiteoak Canyon Run!

_____
10 POINTS

(Listen and look for the stream---on the right of the trail.)
SPECIAL HINT: All the water in this stream is flowing to your destination. It is heading to an **awesome waterfall**! Onward and downward!

⓭

Find the Octopus in the Woods!

_____
10 POINTS

(On the left---close to the trail---just before the footbridge over the stream)
SPECIAL HINT: This tree grew out of and around an old stump. Gradually the **old stump rotted away** and created this octopus tree!

⓮

Find 3 Awesome Trees that Indians & Pioneers Counted On for Building a Fire!

(Just before the trail leads to water cascading over the rocks---on the right of the trail)
SPECIAL HINT: Look for 3 trees that have **yellowish/silverish shiny bark** that is **peeling like shredded paper**. These are **yellow birch trees** and that shredding bark has oil in it! When all the trees in the forest were wet, pioneers and Indians would use this tree to build a fire because even when this tree is wet it will burn due to the oil in the bark! Awesome!

_____
10 POINTS

15

Find a Fallen Hemlock Tree!

10 POINTS

(Hike quite a while---walk through an opening in the cut trunk---you can't miss it.)
SPECIAL HINT: You will walk right through this hemlock tree that fell across the trail. Some of the huge **hemlocks** in this forest were **300-400 years old** before they were killed by a tiny insect from Asia.

16

Find the Museum of Ancient Art!

10 POINTS

(On the right of the trail---as the trail heads down---look for a tree stump's roots sticking straight up---about as tall as a basketball hoop---about 10 feet high.)
SPECIAL HINT: This **tree's roots** look like some kind of really cool art sculpture! With each new sunrise Shenandoah National Park paints a new masterpiece! This is the sculpture section of this awesome forest museum!

17

Find a Giant Boulder Big Enough To Make You Say, "WOW"!

10 POINTS

(On the left---as you go down a hill)
SPECIAL HINT: This giant **greenstone** boulder was once **black lava rock**. It was then re-heated and put under tremendous pressure under the ocean that was here and it eventually turned into greenstone. If you could look inside the rock you would see that it is really dark green on the inside. It has weathered to gray on the outside. Wow!

REMEMBER . . . ALL ROCKS ARE PROTECTED IN THIS NATIONAL PARK.

⑱

Find a Humongous Boulder as Big as a Yacht!

———
10 POINTS

(On the right of the trail)
SPECIAL HINT: This boulder is as big as a yacht! You'll know you found it when someone says, "That's got to be it! It's as big as a yacht!"

⑲

Find the Bridge to the Waterfall!

———
10 POINTS

(Up ahead)
SPECIAL HINT:
This area above the falls was a huge party zone for visitors in the late 1800s and early 1900s. **The owner/ manager of Skyland Resort, George F. Pollock, built a "swimming pool" here** complete with a stand for the orchestra. There were even changing rooms. Food and supplies were carried down by Skyland employees. George was famous for his parties. Party on!

⑳

Find the Hitching Post!

———
10 POINTS

(You can't miss it . . . a post to hitch your horse.)
SPECIAL HINT: Horses from Skyland stables bring visitors down here to see the waterfall! One horse, Sugarfoot, loves lemonade and french fries! Don't you wish you could rent a horse right now so you could ride out of the canyon! Good idea, huh?

㉑

Find the 86-Foot- High Waterfall!

(Don't cross the stream---veer left and follow the trailpost sign to the waterfall---near the flat rock area on the right.)
SPECIAL HINT: Wow! Welcome to upper Whiteoak Falls! Have a picnic, take a break, take a photo (or 2 or 3), eat a snack, take a nap, relax, and take in this incredible view!!! If you continue going down into the canyon you

will find **5 other waterfalls** but you will have to hike a total of 10.6 miles roundtrip! It gets pretty steep and rocky down there (understatement!!!) **Remember . . . if you hike down into the canyon . . . you have to hike back out.** Take your time going back up the trail to your car. Take lots of breaks and enjoy the trip out!

10 POINTS

HEAD LEFT BACK UP THE TRAIL! CONTINUE HIKING ON WHITEOAK FALLS TRAIL TO THE PARKING LOT WHERE YOUR CAR IS!

CONGRATULATIONS!

You have just completed a
SHENANDOAH NATIONAL PARK
SCAVENGER HIKE ADVENTURE!

Whiteoak Canyon Trail to the First Waterfall

10 Points for Each Item Found

TOTAL SCORE: _____

CERTIFIED ACHIEVEMENT LEVEL: _____

over **80** to **100** points: **City Slicker**

over **100** to **140** points: **Pioneer Scout**

over **140** points: **Frontier Explorer**

Name(s):_____

Witness(es) thereof:_____

Date:_____

6

Scavenger Hike Adventure

EXTREME

6.6 MILES ROUNDTRIP

4-5 HOURS

Browns Gap Trail Loop to Upper and Lower Doyles River Falls and Jones Run Falls and Return Via Appalachian Trail

Why This is a Great Trail! This Extreme Scavenger Hike Adventure has all the ingredients you could ever want for an *awesome* Shenandoah experience!!! You will find **3** of the major waterfalls in Shenandoah National Park: **Upper Doyles River Falls**, **Lower Doyles River Falls,** and **Jones Run Falls**! You will find some of the **largest tulip trees** you will ever see in your entire life! On this Scavenger Hike Adventure you will find a **lone gravestone of a Civil War soldier**. You will find **deep pools of water and cascades** as you go down to the bottom of the gorge. You will find an **old road used by Stonewall Jackson's troops** and signs of a major flash flood. This hike is almost always shaded and much of it is alongside mountain streams. This Scavenger Hike Adventure is a great recipe for a great adventure!

Where's the Trail? The trailhead is located at Browns Gap at **milepost 83** in the South District of the park. There is parking for about 12 cars at Browns Gap on the west side of Skyline Drive.

About the Trail: This is an **EXTREME** Scavenger Hike Adventure! It is a loop that includes an old pioneer road, Doyles River Trail, Jones Run Falls Trail, and then back to Browns Gap on the Appalachian Trail. It has sections that are steep, rocky, level, and areas around falls that deserve high caution. A hiking stick is highly recommended for balance on this trail. **CAUTION! WET ROCKS CAN BE AS SMOOTH AND SLIPPERY AS ICE!**

How Long is This Hike? This Scavenger Hike Adventure is a **6.6 mile roundtrip loop** and will take about **4-5 hours!** *oops.*

Things To Hunt For

(Earn 10 points for each treasure you find.)

❶ Find the Old Road Used by General Stonewall Jackson During the Civil War!

10 POINTS

(Cross Skyline Drive from the Browns Gap parking area---STOP at the sign for Browns Gap Fire Road---look to the left---do not start hiking yet.)

SPECIAL HINT: In 1862 **Stonewall Jackson** marched his troops through **Browns Gap** on this road. In fact, this old fire road was once a "turnpike" used to carry food and supplies to Richmond. Imagine Civil War troops and horses and buggies traveling along this route. What a difference 145 years or so makes!

❷ Find the Big Old Apple Tree!

10 POINTS

(As soon as you cross Skyline Drive--- on the left at the beginning of the trail)

SPECIAL HINT: There is a big old **apple tree** on the left of the trail and a few others scattered on both sides as you enter the fire road. The Brown family owned a lot of land around here and apple trees are always a clue that **people once lived in the area before it became a national park.**

❸ Find the Single Gravestone of William H. Howard, F Company, 44ᵗʰ Infantry!

(Hike about *5 minutes* down the trail, or about *1/4 mile,* or count *650 steps* and then look around to your left---up a small side path on the left of the trail---about 20 steps up a steep bank---the gravestone is at eye level as you stand on the trail.)

SPECIAL HINT: This **treasure is** challenging to find but is **well worth the effort** when you do. Look to the left for a **short worn path** to this single gravestone standing alone in the woods. The **gravestone** is behind a tree, but you can see it from the old pioneer road you are hiking on. No one knows for sure what happened to this soldier, but it is likely his death was associated with the **Civil War**.

10 POINTS

❹ Find the Huge Grapevines that Look Like Pretzels!

(Hike a while---look on the left of the trail---growing on an oak tree---right next to the trail---40 steps before a small clearing on the left---where the trail slightly jogs to the right.)

SPECIAL HINT: You will hike for quite a while. *The key clue is the small clearing on the left of the trail just 40 steps past the grapevines.* The clearing will be easily noticed. The vines grew together like pretzels. They are braided at the bottom of the trunk and then twisted like pretzels up in the tree.

10 POINTS

❺ Find a Towering Giant Tulip Tree!

(Hike a while---on the right---about 8 feet from the edge of the trail---**you can't miss it.**)

SPECIAL HINT: **You will hike a while heading down toward Doyles River Trail**. You will know this tree when you see it! It has at least **4 giant branches** heading every which way! **It will make you gasp!** Now you can understand how a pioneer could make an entire log cabin from just one **yellow poplar tree** (**tulip tree**)! If you can look to the top and find a leaf you will notice they are shaped like tulips. This tree has **many trunks** and is a giant of the forest! Wow!!!

10 POINTS

❻ Find Doyles River!

(Under the bridge---under your feet)

SPECIAL HINT: **Doyles River** sometimes looks more like a creek at this point in the trail depending on the amount of rain. You will leave the Browns Gap Fire Road and be sure to **turn right on Doyles River Trail**. The old fire road continues on to the edge of the national park and a left turn on Doyles River Trail

at this intersection will lead to the **Loft Mountain Campground.** Wrong way!

TAKE A RIGHT TURN AFTER THE BRIDGE AND HEAD DOWN INTO THE GORGE ON DOYLES RIVER TRAIL! CHECK THE CONCRETE TRAILPOST!

_____
10 POINTS

❼

Find the Giant Horned Trees!

(Up ahead---on the left and the right of the trail)
SPECIAL HINT: **Hemlock** trees love to live near water and this area was once *really really* shaded by the branches of needles of these big beautiful trees! **When these trees were alive the lower branches of needles dropped off because they couldn't get enough sunlight.** The upper branches got lots of sunlight and the trees continued to grow tall . . . really tall! **The branches where the needles dropped off look like horns!** A tiny insect from Asia, smaller than the tip of a needle, has killed almost all of the hemlock trees in Shenandoah National Park.

_____
10 POINTS

❽

Find a Way To Cross The Next Stream!

(Large boulders crossing the stream)
SPECIAL HINT: When the river is high these boulders will be very helpful. *A wet boulder is as slippery as solid ice on your driveway at home*—or if you live in the south, as slippery as the frozen ice on the driveways of your relatives up north. Be careful!

_____
10 POINTS

❾

Find the Doorway Leading to Upper Doyles River Falls!

(Count 26 steps from the spot where you see a pool of water below a small waterfall.)
SPECIAL HINT: Just ahead, trees "frame" your entrance to the area of **Upper Doyles River Falls.** Look up!

_____
10 POINTS

Find Upper Doyles River Falls!

10

(After a sharp right turn away from the river---go up the small hill---then down to the viewing point.)

SPECIAL HINT: The **upper falls** has 3 tiers or steps and is an awesome **28 feet high**! It is less than half as high as the lower falls, but in the spring this waterfall will knock your socks off! You can get close, but be very careful.

10 POINTS

RETRACE YOUR STEPS BACK TO THE TRAIL.

Find and Hike Around a Group of Boulders as Big as a House!

11

(No special clue needed)
SPECIAL HINT: These boulders are **greenstone**. They were once **black lava rock**, but then were heated up again and under tremendous pressure turned into greenstone, the **most common rock in the park**. The inside of the boulder is dark green.

ALL ROCKS, BOULDERS, PLANTS, AND ANIMALS IN SHENANDOAH NATIONAL PARK ARE PROTECTED BY LAW.

10 POINTS

SAFETY NOTE: PLEASE PUT YOUR BOOK AWAY UNTIL YOU REACH THE NEXT WATERFALL. THERE ARE SOME STEEP BANKS IN THE SECTION AHEAD.

⑫ Find Lower Doyles River Falls!

(Where the trail takes a sharp turn to the right)
SPECIAL HINT: **Lower Doyles River Falls** is **63 feet high**. As you leave the falls and head down the hill, be sure to turn back and see an even better view.

BE CAREFUL! ROCKS ARE EXTREMELY SLIPPERY AROUND THE FALLS AND ON THIS SECTION OF THE TRAIL.

10 POINTS

⑬ Find a Wooden Bridge Deep in the Canyon!

(Crossing a stream flowing into Doyles River)
SPECIAL HINT: Notice that you may be feeling closed in a bit by the mountain walls around you as you reach the bottom of **Doyles River Canyon**!

10 POINTS

⑭ Find Jones Run Trail!

(At the next trail intersection with a concrete marker)
SPECIAL HINT: Wow! You have reached the bottom of the canyon and will now hike out through **Jones Run**! It will be steep, but once you get to the falls it will be much easier. *Take plenty of breaks along the way.* There are beautiful pools of water and areas to relax. Soooooo . . . as you hike out of this canyon, take it easy!

CROSS THE NEXT STREAM WITH CARE.

10 POINTS

⑮ Find the Sign of Flash Floods!

(Tree branches, logs, and debris stuck in the rocks—in Jones Run)
SPECIAL HINT: The steep walls and narrow canyon here mean that in a severe rainstorm the water gathers and flows off the walls of the canyon into this narrow gorge. It can turn into a raging river of whitewater and rapids. The **debris and logs and branches** left here are signs of a **flash flood** that hurled down this canyon. Wow!!!

10 POINTS

⓰
Find Another Humongous Tulip Tree!

_____
10 POINTS

(Hike quite a while---don't look for it---it will find you--- smack dab on the trail.)

SPECIAL HINT: This **giant tulip tree** is 27 size 9.5 hiking boots around its trunk! You will practically hike into this tree so don't worry about searching for it. Just don't bump your head! Be sure to take a minute and find the top of this giant tree!

⓱
Find a Reason To Take a Break!

_____
10 POINTS

(A flat rock, a small, quiet pool of water, a bush, a flower, or need for a drink or snack)

SPECIAL HINT: **Any excuse will do!** Mountain hikers, Mark and Macaroni Clark call **it HOOF time (Hours Outside On Feet**_)!_ _You need to get off your feet._ It will be a good idea to work your way out of this canyon with **lots of breaks**. There are beautiful cascades to explore and photos to take! Enjoy the journey out of this steep canyon. There is an incredible waterfall waiting for you up ahead!

⓲
Find Jones Run Falls!

_____
10 POINTS

(Listen for the sound of water flowing.)

SPECIAL HINT: **Jones Run Falls** drops **42 feet** across a rockface lined with flowers, moss, plants, and butterflies especially in the summer! It looks like a beautiful rock garden! There are large flat boulders at the bottom of the falls—a great place to _sit a spell_ and enjoy this unusual site.

BE CAREFUL ON THE ROCKS! THEY ARE VERY SLIPPERY!

⑲

Find the Overhanging Boulder!

_____
10 POINTS

(As you leave the falls---head up the hill---on the right.)
SPECIAL HINT: In a thunderstorm it might be tempting to rest under an overhang like this. **Don't!!! Lightning** loves the opening between the overhang and the ground. It is an **unsafe place during a thunder storm!**

⑳

Find a Giant Long Rock "Seal"!

_____
10 POINTS

(You will nearly walk into the "seal's" head as it "swims" to the left onto the trail.)
SPECIAL HINT: This is an incredible area of boulders around you. As you wind through them you will notice one that is **shaped like a swimming seal!**

㉑

Find the Hypnotic Cascade!

_____
10 POINTS

(Count 62 steps past the seal and look upstream---on the right.)
SPECIAL HINT: The water in this beautiful **cascade** seems to float down the rockface into a small quiet pool. There is another view of this cascade around the corner up the hill a bit.

㉒

Find a Stream Crossing!

_____
10 POINTS

(Hike a long while.)
SPECIAL HINT: You are getting close to the **Appalachian Trail**.

THE MOST CHALLENGING PART OF THIS ADVENTURE IS BEHIND YOU! NICE JOB!

㉓

Find the Champion Inside You & the Appalachian Trail!

_____
10 POINTS

(Check the concrete marker for the Appalachian Trail--- head north.)
SPECIAL HINT: **Take a right turn (north) on the AT** and enjoy a level, soft, grassy **1.2-mile** cakewalk **to the Browns Gap parking area.** You will enjoy "level" hiking more than you ever dreamed! Enjoy the easy walk to your car on the AT. (Today it stands for "Almost Through!")

CONGRATULATIONS!

You have just completed a

SHENANDOAH NATIONAL PARK
SCAVENGER HIKE ADVENTURE!

Browns Gap Trail Loop

10 Points for Each Item Found

TOTAL SCORE: _____

CERTIFIED ACHIEVEMENT LEVEL: _____

over **80** to **150** points: **City Slicker**

over **150** to **170** points: **Pioneer Scout**

over **170** points: **Frontier Explorer**

Name(s):_____

Witness(es) thereof:_____

Date:_____

7

Scavenger Hike Adventure

EASY
1 MILE LOOP
ABOUT 1 HOUR

Blackrock Summit Loop

Why This is a Great Trail! This Scavenger Hike Adventure is an absolute masterpiece! If it was a painting it would be hanging in a famous museum! You will magically reach the summit of **Blackrock Mountain** at **3,092 feet** without hardly even feeling anything "steep." You will find a humongous **mountaintop** made up of **thousands of large broken rocks** and you will stand over **a half mile above the valley** below. You will find **a place for "happy bears,"** zillions of **ferns** bordering the trail, and you will walk through a beautiful tunnel of **mountain laurel**! You will find **a real tree hugger** and the amazing work of the **second largest woodpecker in North America.** You may have heard how **Shenandoah National Park "paints" a masterpiece with each new sunrise.** Take this Scavenger Hike Adventure early in the morning and you can watch it happen! You don't need to bring a brush, paint, or a canvas. Nature has it covered!

Where's the Trail? The trailhead is located on the west side of the Skyline Drive at **mile 84.8** in the South District of the park. There is a parking area for about 20 cars nestled in the forest. There is a sign along Skyline Drive that says, "Blackrock Summit." Start at **Blackrock Trailhead.**

About the Trail: This is an **EASY** trail—not steep hardly at all and is do-able for all ages of explorers. You will hike around the summit on rocks and you should remember that *rattlesnakes enjoy*

follow AP South
"At the trail post, turn Rt.
• Cont. to boulder field. see quartzite patterns
- cont South. around the slope.
• At intersection, turn Left onto the Blackrock Hut Road - Transfoot Rt. fron

on rocks + view

living here. You will come down from the peak on a soft, grassy old fire road. The views from the top are awesome!

How Long is This Hike? This Scavenger Hike Adventure is a **1.0-mile loop** and will **take about an hour**!

Things To Hunt For

(Earn 10 points for each treasure you find.)

①

Find Out How Far It Is to Blackrock Gap & Blackrock Summit!

10 POINTS

(Concrete post on the right---as you enter the trail and head into the forest)
SPECIAL HINT: You'll be hiking for a short distance on **Trayfoot Mountain Trail** before splitting off onto the **Appalachian Trail**. Take your time. It is not that far to the peak. How far is it? Piece of cake!

②

Find the Double Blue Blaze!

10 POINTS

(On a tree---left of the yellow-chained gate)
SPECIAL HINT: One blue rectangle (called a "blue blaze") painted on a tree indicates that this is an official Shenandoah National Park trail for hikers. Two blue blazes painted on a tree mean that there is a turn in the trail up ahead! **Trayfoot Mountain Trail** was once an old fire road. In fact, if you were to stay on that trail it would pass by the foundation of an old fire watchtower.

③

Find a Berry Happy Black Bear Place!

(Count 30 steps past the chained gate---on the right side of the trail.)
SPECIAL HINT: Bears love **blackberries** and this is a blackberry patch on the right. If they are ripe, it is OK to eat the blackberries while you are here on the trail, but please leave some for the bears! Blackberry plants have thorns so that deer and bears and other animals won't *eat the vines* before the berry blossoms bloom. **Give yourself 5**

bonus points if you find a bear! Bears sometimes sit on branches up in the trees. Look up!

NEVER RUN FROM A BEAR! NEVER TURN YOUR BACK ON A BEAR! GATHER CLOSE TOGETHER WITH YOUR FELLOW EXPLORERS SO THE BEAR WILL THINK YOU ARE ONE BIG ANIMAL. WHEN BEARS ARE BORN THEY ARE ABOUT THE SIZE OF A CAN OF SODA, BUT THEY GROW REALLY FAST!

10 POINTS

4

Find a Fantastic Field of Ferns!

10 POINTS

(On the right side of the trail---as you head up the hill)
SPECIAL HINT: There are about **60 different kinds of ferns** in Shenandoah National Park, but who's counting? One . . . two . . .

5

Find a Mystery of Nature!

(Search for 2 trees with curved trunks---on the right of the trail---as you go up the hill---nearly to the top of the trail.)
SPECIAL HINT: Something happened here a long time ago and caused these **2 tree trunks** to **slightly bend and grow to the right**! You can tell they started bending at the same time, for some reason. If you can't find them, **count 74 steps back from the Appalachian Trail marker ahead** and then look around. Something happened here. What it is . . . isn't exactly clear. Ask a ranger to solve this mystery of the slightly bent trees.

10 POINTS

6

Find the Appalachian Trail (AT) & Go South!

10 POINTS

(Check the trail marker ahead.)

SPECIAL HINT: You could bear to the left, bear straight, or bear right! Straight will lead you *straight* to the summit.

If you take a right, that would lead *you right* to Pennsylvania, New Hampshire, and eventually Maine. Sometimes we kid . . .
but that is not a joke!

7

Find the Mountain Laurel Tunnel!

10 POINTS

(Count 20 steps past the AT trail marker---on the left and right of the trail.)

SPECIAL HINT: **Mountain laurel** wood was used by Indians and pioneers to make spoons. That is why it was also called "**spoonwood**." The **short somewhat shiny leaves** are evergreen and feel sort of **leathery**. Mountain laurel's beautiful **star-shaped** red-to-pink-to-white **flowers** grow in clusters and bloom in the spring. Beautiful!

REMEMBER. . . NEVER HARM A PLANT. EVERY SINGLE PLANT IN THIS NATIONAL PARK IS PROTECTED BY LAW.

8

Find a Tree With Packets of 5!

10 POINTS

(Hike along the left side of the trail---the tree will tickle your arm---it is about 10 steps before a tree with a painted white blaze/rectangle.)

SPECIAL HINT: This small **white pine** tree is on the left side of the trail. You will almost brush your left shoulder against it. Look very closely at the **long, soft needles.** *They come in little packets of 5 needles each.* You can now officially identify a white pine tree!

9
Find a Tree Hugging Another Tree!

10 POINTS

(Count 22 steps past the tree with the 5 packets of needles---on the right---next to the trail---on the ground.)
SPECIAL HINT: Look at ground level. This *really* is a tree hugger!

10
Find the Holes Made by a Giant Woodpecker!

10 POINTS

(On the left---on a dead tree with two limbs sticking up from the ground---as you enter an area scattered with dead trees---this tree almost touches the left side of the trail.)
SPECIAL HINT: The **pileated (pronounced either Pile-ee-ated or Pill-ee-ated) woodpecker** sometimes makes holes large enough to stick your hand inside. Whoa! This is one of the largest woodpeckers in North America and can make *really, really* big holes in the trees. Usually the holes have an oval or rectangular shape to them. Sometimes the woodpecker builds a nest inside the hole. Watch for more pileated woodpecker holes along the trail!

11
Find the Exact Spot Where Someone in Your Group Will Say, "WOW"!

10 POINTS

(Just keep hiking until you hear someone uncontrollably say, "Wow!")
SPECIAL HINT: Your first view of **Blackrock Summit** will knock your hiking socks off! It will take your breath away! It will surprise you! It will do all of those things at once! Blackrock Summit used to be a high cliff, but water kept filling the cracks in the boulders and then kept freezing and thawing. It broke the cliff into thousands of smaller rocks. Can we hear one more "Wow!"?

12
Find the Reason Blackrock is Named "Blackrock"!

(In every direction---look for black speckled rocks.)
SPECIAL HINT: **Rock tripe** is growing everywhere on the rocks and boulders! If someone named this mountain on a rainy day it might have been called *Greenrock* because rock tripe turns green when it is wet. Dry rock tripe looks like dead black/brown

leaves scattered about on the rocks. **Rock Tripe is a lichen (pronounced LIKE-in).** Lichen is a combination of **algae and fungus**. Look for big pieces of rock tripe in the more shaded areas on the rocks.

10 POINTS

⑬
Find a "White Line" in a Rock!

(Count 4 steps past the rock with a white blaze (rectangle) that shows you're still on the Appalachian Trail---on the right---next to the trail.)
SPECIAL HINT: This big area of rocks is called a field of **"talus"** (broken rocks). Find a white strip or **vein of quartz** running around a boulder. This boulder had a crack in it and the quartz was so hot it melted and then flowed into those cracks before cooling down and getting hard. How cool is that?

BEWARE OF SNAKES! THEY LOVE TO HANG OUT BETWEEN THE ROCKS ON TALUS SLOPES.

10 POINTS

⑭
Find the Spot That Was Once a Sandy Beach on an Ocean!

(Look underneath your hiking boots.)
SPECIAL HINT: All of these broken-up rocks and boulders are **quartzite**! About **570 million years ago** (give or take a couple of years) this area was a sandy ocean beach. It is kind of hard to picture that right now, but it is true! The tiny little pieces of **sandstone** on that ancient beach had **quartz** in it. Later, volcanic **lava** and high temperatures heated that beach sand and the heat and pressure turned it into humongous very hard boulders. **Blackrock Summit** was once just one big giant hunk of quartzite until water kept freezing and thawing over and over again in the cracks, breaking it into these rocks. Go ahead—pet one of these rocks. They have had a long tough journey to end up right here under your feet!

10 POINTS

15

Find the Miniature Trees!

10 POINTS

(As you curve left around the summit)
SPECIAL HINT: The **weather and wind are really extreme** at **3,092 feet** elevation! These trees have learned it is better to just stay closer to the ground where it is not quite so windy and a bit warmer in the winter. You won't find any tall trees up here this high.

16

Find a White Pine Tree!

10 POINTS

(As you go around the peak---on the right---near the trail marker)
SPECIAL HINT: Remember, the long soft green needles are in packets of 5.

NOTE: AT THIS MARKER, WHICH IS HALF-WAY AROUND BLACKROCK SUMMIT, BE SURE TO JUST KEEP ON GOING AROUND THE SUMMIT. DON'T GO RIGHT. THAT WOULD BE WRONG.

17

Find the Way Back to Your Car!

10 POINTS

(At the next trail intersection---and trail marker)
SPECIAL HINT: As you finish going around the summit, you'll see another trail marker a little ways ahead on the trail. **Go left** on **Trayfoot Mountain Trail** to head to your car. You will be following the soft and grassy old fire road down the mountain.

18

Find a Tree Stump & Calculate the Age of the Tree!

(Stumps on the left and the right--- please stay on the trail.)
SPECIAL HINT: Each ring on the stump is one year of growth! To **calculate the approximate age** of this tree, turn your "**pointing finger**" into a tree **age measuring device**:

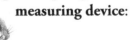

1. Lay your **pointing finger** on the edge of the stump with your pointing finger's **knuckle** at the outer first tree ring.

2. Count the number of rings from the **tip of your finger to your knuckle**.

3. Now put your **other pointing finger on that knuckle . . .** that is your **measuring device**.

4. Slide your "measuring device" to the center of the tree, **counting how many fingertip to knuckle moves you make.**

5. **Multiply that** times the number of rings you counted in step #2.

10 POINTS

⑲

Find Burnt Trees that Have Turned to Black Charcoal from a Fire Here Along This Trail!

10 POINTS

(Look on both sides of the trail.)

SPECIAL HINT: You just might want to pick up a small piece of charcoal and write a short message to yourself. Please be sure to put the charcoal back where it came from.

REMEMBER . . . NEVER TAKE ANYTHING FROM SHENANDOAH NATIONAL PARK. EVERYTHING IS PROTECTED HERE.

BE SURE TO FOLLOW SIGNS BACK TO THE BLACKROCK TRAILHEAD PARKING LOT.

CONGRATULATIONS!

You have just completed a
SHENANDOAH NATIONAL PARK
SCAVENGER HIKE ADVENTURE!

Blackrock Summit Loop

10 Points for Each Item Found
TOTAL SCORE: _____
CERTIFIED ACHIEVEMENT LEVEL: _____

over **80** to **100** points: **City Slicker**
over **100** to **130** points: **Pioneer Scout**
over **130** points: **Frontier Explorer**

Name(s): _____

Witness(es) thereof: _____

_____

Date: _____

8
Scavenger Hike Adventure

EXTREME

6.8 MILES ROUNDTRIP

ABOUT 5 HOURS

Jewell Hollow Overlook to Marys Rock Summit

Why This is a Great Trail! This Scavenger Hike Adventure is filled with **incredible treasures** from start to finish! It is like a treasure chest! You will find an amazing super **huge boulder balancing itself on top of another boulder,** a beautiful **tree that will *never ever* grow old,** an **awesome view of famous Stony Man Mountain,** and a **gray ghost!** Locals say this stretch of trail has the **best views of the Shenandoah Valley** and you will say the same thing . . . absolutely guaranteed! You will find **giant ferns,** a **hidden camping spot** for thru-hikers, and even **a tree that is wearing a cowboy boot!** You will hike through the middle of a massive field of **truck-sized boulders**! Just when you think you can't handle any more beauty or awesome sights, you arrive at the **breathtaking pinnacle of Marys Rock**! Whew!!!

Where's the Trail? The trailhead is located on the west side of the Skyline Drive at **mile 36.4** at Jewell Hollow Overlook in the Central District of the park. The trail begins at the south end of the overlook.

About the Trail: This is an **EXTREME** Scavenger Hike Adventure! It is uphill, downhill, strenuous, rocky, grassy, with stunning vista views—and more! This is a great spring or fall hike. It could be quite hot and buggy in the summer so you'd want to start early in the morning. Some locals say this section of the AT has the best views in the entire national park!!!

How Long is This Hike? This Scavenger Hike Adventure is **6.8 miles roundtrip** and will take **about 5 hours**. This is a great early morning hike.

Things To Hunt For

(Earn 10 points for each treasure you find.)

① Find the Water Catchers for Jewell Hollow!

(At the overlook--- down at the bottom of Jewell Hollow--- look toward the left.)

SPECIAL HINT: When it rains the water runs down **Jewell Hollow** like a funnel and the dam below catches the water for the farmers and other folks living way down there. By the way, **Jewell Hollow Overlook** is at the intersection of 3 different counties. Years ago if an outlaw was being chased by a county sheriff, he could just move across 1 county line to another—where that sheriff had no authority to arrest him! That rule doesn't work today!

10 POINTS

② Find the Water Fountain that Used To Work!

(At the start of the trail---on the left---look for a steel water pipe and faucet.)

SPECIAL HINT: The **Civilian Conservation Corps** built water fountains, trails, bridges, rock walls, and picnic grounds in Shenandoah National Park. The Civilian Conservation Corps **(CCC)** was created to give jobs to unemployed young men in the 1930s. They made $30 each month and $25 of it was sent back home to their families. The **CCC** boys built this old water fountain. The **CCC** boys were sometimes called the "**Tree Army**" because they also planted billions of trees around the U.S!

10 POINTS

③ Find the Marker Showing the Way to Marys Rock!

(Hike 50 feet to the Appalachian Trail.)

SPECIAL HINT: When you reach the **Appalachian Trail**, be sure to head toward **Marys Rock**. Check the trail sign carefully!

10 POINTS

❹ Find Some Bear Scat!

(Look along the trail up ahead as you hike below the Jewell Hollow Overlook---go on to #5 as you look.)

SPECIAL HINT: This huge field of **berries** is probably well-known by every bear within 30 miles. Berry bushes are on both sides of the trail below the **Jewell Hollow Overlook**. In the summer you will find bear droppings (called scat) all along this trail. The scat varies from black to brown and can be tapered or flat on the ends or sometimes even just one big clump. **Bear scat** will usually "show" what the bear has been eating. Go on to #5 as you continue to keep your eye out for bears and bear scat! Time to scat!

NEVER TOUCH BEAR SCAT. IF YOU ARE CURIOUS ABOUT WHAT THE BEAR HAS BEEN EATING, POKE IT WITH A STICK.

10 POINTS

❺ Find a Giant Oak Tree with 3 Trunks!

10 POINTS

(Near the intersection with the Leading Ridge Trail---on the right---next to the trail---as you go up the hill---head straight ahead on the AT toward Thornton Gap.)

SPECIAL HINT: This big old giant oak tree is magnificent! When it was a young sapling something happened to it to cause it to grow **3 trunks**. It could have been an animal gnawing on the trunk, wind breaking it, lightning, or even disease. In the 1990s **gypsy moth caterpillars** found the oak trees in Shenandoah and killed many of them by eating their leaves. **Cuckoo birds** somehow learned that the gypsy moth caterpillars were here and some fly to Shenandoah to eat them. Cuckoo birds go cuckoo over gypsy moth caterpillars! Everything is pretty much OK now.

6

Find the Rock Bed!

10 POINTS

(On the right of the trail)
SPECIAL HINT: This flat boulder is about the size of a full-size bed. If you prefer a very firm mattress, this is a great spot to take a nap. It is not *bedrock!* It is a *rock bed!*

7

Find the Young Tree that Will Never Grow Old!

10 POINTS

(Count 54 steps past the rock bed---on the right.)
SPECIAL HINT: This young chestnut tree has large feather-shaped leaves (about 6-12 inches long). This tree will never grow old! Chestnut trees were once the main tree in Shenandoah. About 50% of the trees were chestnuts! Sadly, a **fungus came here in the 1900s** and killed almost all of the **American chestnut** trees. Young trees still sprout up, but once they reach about 20 feet tall they are killed by the fungus. Chestnut trees once grew to over 100 feet tall and 10 feet in diameter. So far, no one can figure out how to stop the fungus.

8

Find Rock Tripe Village!

(Hike a while---up ahead on the left and right of the trail.)
SPECIAL HINT: So many of the boulders are covered with **rock tripe** it looks like it should be called **Rock Tripe Village**! Rock tripe **looks like** crumpled up **dead leaves** on the rocks. Many of the boulders here are as big as Volkswagon Beetles, pick-up trucks, and even houses! Rock tripe is a combination of **algae and fungus** called **lichen (pronounced LIKE-in)**. It is a favorite snack of **flying squirrels** and **George Washington** fed it to his troops at Valley Forge when regular food was scarce. Some say after it is boiled it tastes like a bitter combination of licorice and tapioca. It also sometimes causes cramps and other not-so-good aftereffects. If you could choose between

blackberry cobbler with vanilla ice cream . . . or a bowl of rock tripe . . . **we highly recommend the cobbler!**

ALL LICHEN IS PROTECTED IN THE PARK. DO NOT EAT THE ROCK TRIPE!

10 POINTS

❾

Find a Humongous Boulder Balanced on Another Boulder!

(Look on the right as you go up the hill--- about 15 steps to the right of the trail---on a faint side path---in Rock Tripe Village.)
SPECIAL HINT: **You will not want to miss this treasure!** Peer into the woods on the right! If you have a camera you will definitely use it here! This **amazing balanced boulder** looks like it is being held up by a young **birch tree**. There is a faint **side path** leading to the boulder.

REMEMBER THAT RATTLESNAKES LIKE TO LIVE AMONG ROCKS AND BOULDERS . . . SO JUST BE ALERT!

10 POINTS

❿

Find the Gray Ghost!

(Hike a while---on the right of the trail---so close to the trail *your right shoulder might touch it*---after the trail levels---just before the pinnacle view.)
SPECIAL HINT: **Dead chestnut trees** and other dead trees sometimes turn gray or white and in the evening moonlight pioneers thought they looked like **gray ghosts** against the dark sky! Look for the small **birch tree** that is growing out of the trunk of the dead tree. If you reach the pinnacle view, you have just passed a gray ghost! Keep your eyes wide open for more ghostly appearances up ahead along this trail!

10 POINTS

⑪ Find an Incredible Pinnacle View!

10 POINTS

(On the left---near the small opening)
SPECIAL HINT: *Be careful on the rocks!*
This is just **one of many incredible views** along the ridge on this section of the **AT**. Pretty awesome, huh?

⑫ Find a Sign of the Largest Forest Fire in the National Park's History!

10 POINTS

(Look all along the way---to the Byrds Nest Hut.)
SPECIAL HINT: You will be hiking a while now until you reach the day shelter. Look for **black stumps** or **charred logs** that still show the remains of the **largest forest fire** Shenandoah National Park ever had!

⑬ Find a White Blaze (Rectangle) on a Tree!

10 POINTS

(Look on the trees along the trail.)
SPECIAL HINT: This **white blaze** means you are still hiking on the **AT!**

⑭ Find an Empty Water Pipe Crossing the Trail!

10 POINTS

(Just before you reach Byrds Nest #3 Hut)
SPECIAL HINT: This brown pipe blends right in with the trail. It was used to carry water to the shelter from a spring that is farther up the hill behind you.

⑮ Find a Barbeque Pit!

10 POINTS

(Near the shelter)
SPECIAL HINT: This hut is a great place to take a break! **Harry F. Byrd, Sr.,** donated materials for the 4 day shelters in the park, all known as Byrds Nests. He was the **governor of Virginia and a U.S. senator.** Recently Byrds Nest #3 was converted to a hut for long-distance hikers.

16

Find More Gray Ghosts!

10 POINTS

(On the left of the trail)
SPECIAL HINT: There are many tall dead tree stumps here along the trail. Imagine a clear night with a full moon! These gray ghosts would look awesome in the moonlight!

17

Find the Coolest Hidden Camping Spot You've Ever Seen!

10 POINTS

(At the next viewpoint to the west---side path to the left)
SPECIAL HINT: This **peaceful camping spot** will make you want to hike the AT just so you could set up camp here! Imagine setting up your pup tent, having a bite to eat, and watching the sun disappear below you. Look straight out to a mountain with a "V" shape in the middle. This is 40-mile-long **Massanutten Mountain!** We have added this spot to our list of "to-do's."

BY THE WAY, BE SURE TO HEAD LEFT AS YOU HEAD OUT TO RETURN TO THE TRAIL FROM THE SIDE PATH.

18

Find the Small Tunnel through a Humongous Pile of Boulders!

10 POINTS

(On the left of the trail)
SPECIAL HINT: Look closely! In this giant pile of rocks is a hole that goes all the way through this pile of boulders. **Black bears** might den among these rocks in the winter! There are somewhere between **300-500 black bears** in Shenandoah National Park!

ALWAYS KEEP YOUR DISTANCE FROM ALL WILDLIFE! NEVER FEED WILD ANIMALS IN THE PARK! IF YOU SEE A BEAR . . . STAY CALM . . . BACK AWAY . . . STAY WITH YOUR HIKING GROUP, AND GIVE THE BEAR LOTS OF SPACE! NEVER RUN! USUALLY MAKING NOISE SUCH AS CLAPPING YOUR HANDS WILL SEND THE BEAR ON ITS WAY!

19

Find a Balancing Boulder!

10 POINTS

(On the left---as the trail turns right)
SPECIAL HINT: This boulder likely weighs hundreds or maybe even thousands of pounds and it is balanced on a spot about the size of a large dinner platter.
Amazing!

20

Find a View of Stony Man Mountain!

10 POINTS

(Count 61 steps past the awesome balancing boulder---look around---viewpoint on the left.)
SPECIAL HINT: *Be careful at this viewing point! It is wonderful, but dangerous!* If you look to the far left you can see **Stony Man Mountain!** It is a profile of a man's forehead, eyes, nose, mouth, and beard. If you hike to Stony Man, the destination spot for your hike is actually the "forehead." Do you see anyone standing on Stony Man's forehead?

21

Find a Trail Marker that Leads to Meadow Springs!

10 POINTS

(Continue straight on the AT, actually veer a little to the left, at this trail intersection.)
SPECIAL HINT: Go straight (actually veer a slight left) at this intersection! The trail to the right goes about a half mile before reaching Skyline Drive. There is a really awesome chimney from an old cabin down this trail to the right, but stay focused . . . straight ahead to the incredible top of Marys Rock.

22

Find a Tree Wearing a Cowboy Boot!

10 POINTS

(On the left---as you go up the mountain---close to the trail)
SPECIAL HINT: The bottom of this tree grew around a rock and looks like this tree is wearing a cowboy boot! The boot's toe is pointing back downhill from Marys Rock.

㉓

Find Ferns that Grow About 4 to 5 Feet High!

---

10 POINTS

(On the right of the trail---after the trail levels out)
SPECIAL HINT: These **ferns** grow up to 5 feet high and are really spectacular! In the fall they will turn orange-ish brown.

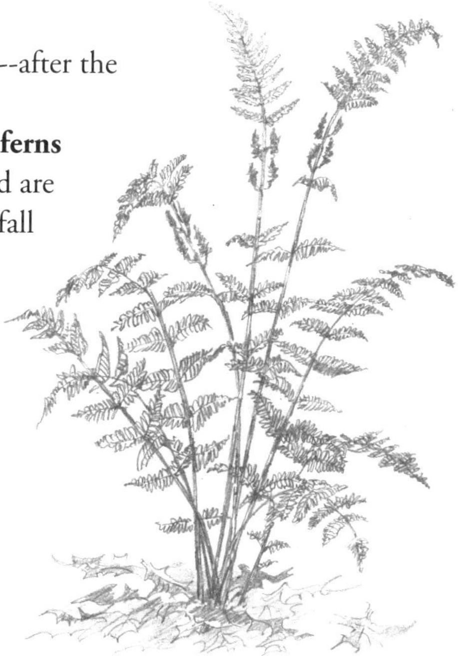

㉔

Find Pedro & Jeff's Rock!

---

10 POINTS

(On the left of the trail---flat connected boulders)
SPECIAL HINT: *Be careful! Sheer cliff drops here!* The first time we hiked this trail we came upon Pedro and Jeff sitting here enjoying the view. They welcomed us to **"Marys Rock."** They thought it was awesome! Well, Pedro and Jeff actually missed the turn down the hill and they *thought* they were sitting on **Marys Rock. NOT!!!** We promised we would name this viewpoint after them and then we all hiked together from "Pedro and Jeff's Rock" to the real Marys Rock!

㉕

Find a Double White Blaze on Another Balancing Boulder!

---

10 POINTS

(On the right---before the AT turns to the right)
SPECIAL HINT: You are definitely getting close now!

26 Find the Trail Marker for Marys Rock!

(At the next trail intersection)

SPECIAL HINT: You will now head up the hill just 1/10th of a mile (not far) to the pinnacle of **Marys Rock**!

MAKE A NOTE OF THIS TRAIL MARKER BECAUSE ON THE WAY BACK DOWN IT MAY BE HIDDEN BY BUSHES AND IF YOU MISS IT . . . THIS HIKE COULD BECOME VERY, VERY LONG.

NOTE: ON THE RETURN TRIP YOU MUST WATCH FOR THIS CONCRETE TRAILPOST AND TAKE A RIGHT. LOOK BACK NOW AS YOU HEAD DOWN THE TRAIL AND SEE IF IT IS KIND OF HIDDEN BEHIND THE BUSHES AND A ROCK. IF YOU MISS THIS TURN ON THE WAY BACK, YOU WILL HEAD IN THE WRONG DIRECTION.

10 POINTS

27 Find Marys Rock!

(Top of the mountain)

SPECIAL HINT: **Marys Rock** is a beautiful place to spend some time! There are geological markers at the top of the peak, but *be very careful* if you decide to check it out! Watch for **turkey vultures** soaring *below* you. They just glide in the sky and hardly ever flap their wings. A turkey vulture has a bare red head and a dark body. Oh . . . It is perfectly OK to feel like you are on top of the world right now!

10 POINTS

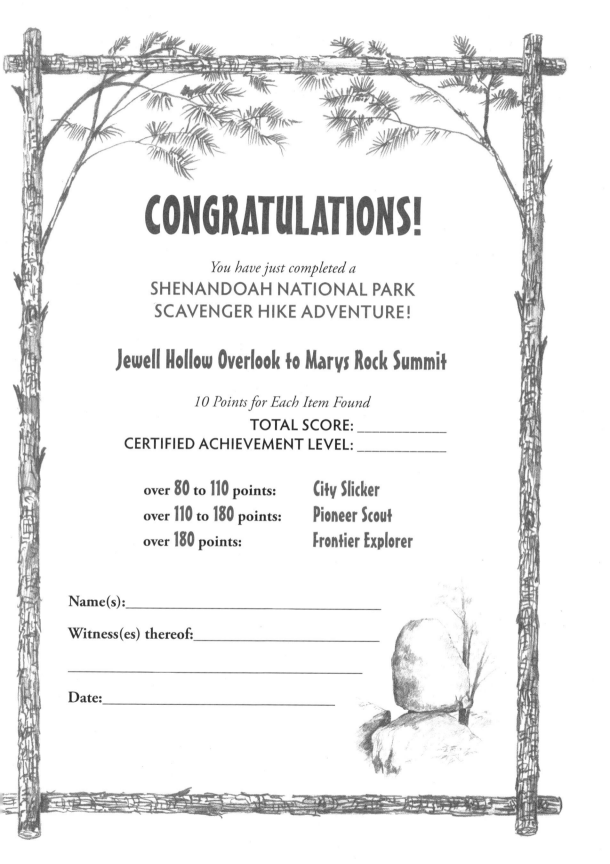

CONGRATULATIONS!

You have just completed a
SHENANDOAH NATIONAL PARK
SCAVENGER HIKE ADVENTURE!

Jewell Hollow Overlook to Marys Rock Summit

10 Points for Each Item Found

TOTAL SCORE: _____

CERTIFIED ACHIEVEMENT LEVEL: _____

over **80** to **110** points: City Slicker

over **110** to **180** points: Pioneer Scout

over **180** points: Frontier Explorer

Name(s):_____

Witness(es) thereof:_____

_____

Date:_____

9

Scavenger Hike Adventure

MODERATE

4 MILE LOOP

4-5 HOURS

Rose River Falls Loop to Rose River Falls and Dark Hollow Falls

Why This is a Great Trail! This incredible Scavenger Hike Adventure leads you through a deep green forest along the beautiful **Rose River**! You will be hiking in **"surround sound"** as you pass zillions of **awesome cascades and waterfalls** all along the way. **Two magnificent waterfalls** plummet from rocky points taller than a 6-story building! Whew!!! You will "march" a bit on the famous **Civil War road** used by **General Stonewall Jackson** and his thousands of troops. You will find the remains of an old abandoned **copper mine** and **holes in a tree** made by the **second largest woodpecker in all of North America!** If that's not enough to knock your hiking socks off . . . then find the **bear claw marks** on a tree that fell across the trail! "A rose by any other name is still a rose," except in this case . . . it is an *awesome* Scavenger Hike Adventure!!!

Where's the Trail? Park at the Fishers Gap Overlook at **mile 49.4** on the west side of Skyline Drive in the Central District of the park. If the parking lot is full, there is additional parking along the Rose River Fire Road just a few steps north of the overlook. This Scavenger Hike Adventure begins at Fishers Gap Overlook.

About the Trail: This is a **MODERATE** trail *with an "attitude"!* It is a little steep in places, but is well worth a little huffin' and puffin'. The hike heads down for a couple of miles and then levels out before heading up out of Dark Hollow! It is great for folks who are looking for a bit of a challenge. Much of the trail is soft dirt with some very rocky, rooty areas. *Remember . . . wet rocks are very slippery.* The **optional side-trail to Dark Hollow Falls** is steep but very short and well worth the trek to this beautiful waterfall!

Bring enough food to picnic next to a waterfall at least once . . . maybe twice!

How Long is This Hike?
This Scavenger Hike Adventure is a **4.0-mile loop** and will take explorers about **4 to 5 hours** including time for 2 picnics and a brief nap.

Things To Hunt For

(Earn 10 points for each treasure you find.)

①
Find the Famous Road Used by General Stonewall Jackson & His Thousands of Troops!

(Stand at the center of the overlook---take 15 steps to the right---look straight out toward Shenandoah Valley far below---then stare at your feet and push your chin up no more than 3 inches.)
SPECIAL HINT: You are now looking at the famous **Civil War road** that **General Stonewall Jackson** used in November of **1862**.
He led his thousands of troops over this mountain after a successful battle against the Union soldiers in the valley below! Just imagine all of those soldiers passing by you at this very spot. The road is now used as a fire road. Look out and find the deep "V"-shaped gap in the 40-mile-long **Massanutten Mountain**. Yes, one Mountain . . . 40 miles long!!!

10 POINTS

②

Find the Symbol on the Marker for a 2,175-Mile-Long Hiking Trail!

10 POINTS

(At the left corner of the overlook)
SPECIAL HINT: The metal band on this concrete marker says that the world-famous **Appalachian Trail** is only 60 yards from this spot (about half the length of a football field). The **AT** runs through forests and over mountains all the way from **Georgia to Maine,** crossing **14 different states!** If you have an extra few months, just follow the painted white rectangles (white blazes), the official mark on trees for the AT. Hiking the AT is a whopper of an adventure! Today . . . your exploration party *probably* should just stick with the original plan.

③

Find the Yellow Rectangle on the Tree!

10 POINTS

(Head back past the overlook where you were just standing---cross the Skyline Drive---follow the Rose River Fire Road for about 100 feet---go 10 steps past the chained posts---look to the left.)
SPECIAL HINT: Horses look for the yellow rectangles on the trees to be sure they are heading in the right direction. The **yellow rectangle** means this is a **horse trail** (people can hike on horse trails, too). Even though you are probably not a horse, follow the yellow brick road. Oh, no . . . we mean follow the yellow blazes . . . sorry . . . wrong forest!!! If this still isn't clear enough . . . go left . . . do not go straight.

④

Find the 9.5-Mile Marker Where Horses Say, "WHOA!!!"

10 POINTS

(On the right of the trail)
SPECIAL HINT: About 20 horses live near **Skyland Resort** and take folks on rides through beautiful Shenandoah National Park! You can bring your own horse if you have one and ride more than **150 miles on horse trails.** At this intersection the horses have already gone 9.5 miles on this trail and are probably amazed to read this marker!

❺

Find a Big Boulder with White Splotches!

_____

10 POINTS

(On the right of the trail---touches the right side of the trail)

SPECIAL HINT: This big boulder is covered with white splotches. You are looking at **lichen (pronounced Like-in).** It is a combination of **algae and fungus** and when it gets wet it makes an acid that after _many many many_ years will break down this rock into soil. Amazing!

❻

Find at Least 3 Holes Made by the Second Largest Woodpecker in North America!

_____

10 POINTS

(Hike a while---count 39 steps past the "Y" intersection in the trail--- look around on the left---at the tree on the ground.)

SPECIAL HINT: The horse trail will bear left at the "Y" intersection and the **Rose River Trail** heads straight on down the hill. _Be sure you go straight._ Although hikers are allowed to go on horse trails . . . _**do not follow the yellow blaze!**_ The **pileated woodpecker (pronounced either Pile-ee-ated or Pill-ee-ated)** is a huge black bird with a bright red crest. It looks like that old cartoon character, Woody Woodpecker! This giant woodpecker sometimes makes large oval holes in trees that are big enough to stick your fist inside! Wow!

❼

Find the Blue Blaze To Be Sure You Are on the Correct Trail!

_____

10 POINTS

(Immediately look for a tree on the left side of the trail.)

SPECIAL HINT: The **blue blaze (rectangle)** tells you this is a Shenandoah National Park **"people" trail**. If you see a herd of horses and yellow blazes, you are lost! If you see the blue blaze . . . beautiful **Rose River** is straight ahead!

8

Find a Chipmunk or a Bear!

(Look all along the trail---go on to #9 as you search.)

SPECIAL HINT: Give yourself **5 bonus points if you find a bear!** A bear track looks like a bare human foot except it has claw marks at the end of each toe. **Bears** will often be high up in trees. **Chipmunks** will be scurrying about gathering seeds in their cheeks and putting them in little chipmunk hiding spots for future meals. Chipmunks can hold over **1,000 grass seeds** at one time in their little cheek pouches!

REMEMBER... NEVER FEED BEARS, CHIPMUNKS, OR ANY WILDLIFE. KEEP YOUR DISTANCE. IF YOU SEE A BEAR ... DO NOT RUN AND DO NOT TURN YOUR BACK ON IT. GIVE IT LOTS OF SPACE. CLAP YOUR HANDS AND MAKE NOISE ... IT WILL USUALLY MOVE ON. FOLLOW THE BEAR PRECAUTIONS IN THE FRONT OF THE BOOK.

10 POINTS

9

Find & Smell Rose River!

(Hike quite a ways---on the left of the trail---you will hear it before you see it.)

SPECIAL HINT: Take a big whiff! **If you smell a "Rose" give yourself 2 bonus points for "imagination."** According to a map in 1795, the river was actually named **"Rows River,"** probably after early pioneers instead of the flower.

Later, someone changed the name or the spelling to "Rose River." If your name is **Rose, Rosie, Rosalind, Rosemond, or Melrose, give yourself 5 extra bonus points.**

10 POINTS

⑩ Find Rose River Falls!

(Hike a while---you will pass many cascades on the way---on the left.)

SPECIAL HINT: Magnificent **Rose River Falls** drops **67 feet** into a beautiful pool of water! Depending on the water level you might even see 3 waterfalls in one! *Now is a really good time to be very careful. Wet rocks are extremely slippery.* Scientists believe that the **negative energy** coming from waterfalls **improves overall health and well-being**. Go ahead and sing it, "I feel good!!!"

10 POINTS

⑪ Find the Strange Snack of Flying Squirrels!

(Above the trail at the falls---growing on the boulders---on the right side of the trail)

SPECIAL HINT: Look up! It **looks like brown leaves** growing on the boulders, but it is really "**rock tripe**," a favorite snack of flying squirrels. Rock tripe turns green when it is wet. It is **"lichen" (pronounced LIKE-in)**, a combination of **algae and fungus. Flying squirrels** have big flaps of skin that connect their front and back feet so they can "glide" like a kite. They don't really fly like a bird. They usually only appear at night. Is it a bird? Is it a plane? No, it is a flying squirrel looking for some rock tripe!

10 POINTS

⑫ Find a Mini-Waterfall!

(Hike quite a ways---you will head away from the river and then back---look for a rock on the right of the trail shaped something like an arrow and about the size of a Lazy Boy reclining chair.)

SPECIAL HINT: The **boulder** you are looking for is so close to the trail you might **brush your leg against it!** If you stand at the boulder and look toward the river you will see a pretty mini-waterfall!

10 POINTS

13

Find a Fallen Tree with 2 Trunks that Was Clawed by a Bear!

(On the right side of the trail--- on the ground---count 265 steps from the arrow-shaped boulder in clue #12---look around.) SPECIAL HINT: Look for a tree with 2 trunks that fell completely across the trail. *A ranger had to cut the tree so you can hike on through.* Find the **swiped claw marks** on the lower trunk section. **Black bears** live in the park. They will search for bugs and grubs in dead logs and will also sometimes **"mark" a tree** (like this one) to let other bears know they should "stay out" of its territory.

_____

10 POINTS

14

Find & Walk on the Site of an Ancient Indian Camp!

(At the very sharp right-hand turn in the trail---left of the concrete trail marker---walk a few steps to the left on the side path.) SPECIAL HINT: **Monacan** and **Manahoac** tribes hunted here in the 1600s. Many of their footpaths went along streams and rivers. You are very likely walking in the exact same steps as those ancient Native Americans. "Walk a while in their moccasins!" There is evidence that American Indians lived in the Shenandoah Valley and used **Big Meadows** as **temporary trading or hunting camps** about **8,000 years ago**. If you are hungry, go ahead and picnic at this ancient Indian camp overlooking the river! An awesome spot!!!

REMEMBER . . . ALWAYS PACK OUT YOUR TRASH . . . PLEASE TAKE IT WITH YOU!

_____

10 POINTS

⑮ Find 8 Bolts & 6 Nuts!

(Smack dab in the middle of the trail)
SPECIAL HINT: A huge hunk of concrete is in the middle of the trail. It once held a piece of mining equipment used in the **copper mine** that was just behind you up the small hill. Look for the small broken chips of blue-gray rocks called **tailings**. They came from the mine. Find the long pipe running along the tailings. The **copper mine was worked from 1845-50**, abandoned, and then **opened up again in 1902.** By the way, the "nut" count does not include members of your hiking group!

REMEMBER . . . NEVER TAKE ANYTHING INCLUDING HISTORIC ARTIFACTS FROM A NATIONAL PARK. EVERYTHING HERE IS PROTECTED BY LAW!

10 POINTS

⑯ Find the Metal Marker on the Bridge over Hogcamp Branch!

(On the handrail---on the left side of the bridge)
SPECIAL HINT: This bridge was built by the **Continental Custom Bridge Company**. The 800 phone number on the marker is still good in case you need to build a bridge. Hey! Fast-moving water flowing over rocks and boulders is called a "**cascade.**" You will see zillions of awesome cascades up ahead.

10 POINTS

⑰ Find a Boulder Bigger than a Volkswagon Beetle!

(On the right---next to the trail)
SPECIAL HINT: This giant boulder has **2 blue blazes** on it so you will know you are on a **Shenandoah National Park hiking trail that is about to make a turn.** Check out the incredible cascade just past this humongous boulder!

10 POINTS

SPECIAL NOTE: HERE IS A SPECIAL MATHEMATICAL FORMULA REGARDING "ENERGY" (KIND OF LIKE THE EINSTEIN THEORY).

MB+S=ME+HH

(More Breaks + Snacks = More Energy + Happy Hikers)

This section is uphill for a bit. Just take your time and take lots of breaks as needed. Coming up . . . a great spot for a picnic by the water!

18

Find a Fish in Hogcamp Branch!

_____
10 POINTS

(At the second sharp left turn---look in the pool at the end of the cascade.)
SPECIAL HINT: **Brook trout** can be caught in the national park, but you *will need a license and will have to follow park rules.* If you don't find a fish here, keep looking all along the way to get the points! Remember the special mathematical formula highlighted above. It is a proven formula created by a mathematical genius. Don't take it lightly! It will get steeper up ahead.
MB+S=ME+HH

19

Find a Big Flat Rock that Is Taking a Break!

_____
10 POINTS

(Crosses practically the whole trail)
SPECIAL HINT: This flat rock is taking a break! You can always learn something from a rock!

20

Find the Awesome Slippery Rock Cascades!

_____
10 POINTS

(Count 120 steps from the rock that was taking a break--- look toward the river---then to your left.)
SPECIAL HINT: These **cascades** are beautiful. Sit awhile and enjoy the magic!

㉑

Find Another Bridge Over Hogcamp Branch!

10 POINTS

(Straight ahead)
SPECIAL HINT: The large metal bridge crossing **Hogcamp Branch** is on the **Rose River Fire Road.** You think *this* is awesome? Wait till you see **Dark Hollow Falls!!!**

Optional:

㉒

Find the Most Visited Waterfall in Shenandoah National Park!

10 POINTS

(After crossing the bridge---the trail heads up the hill to the left.)
SPECIAL HINT: This short side-trail to beautiful **Dark Hollow Falls (70-foot drop)** is very steep but *is worth every single step* of the way! It is only about as far as 1 time around a high school track. You can do it! But, if you can't make it today . . . don't worry . . . it will still be here for you when you come back another time!

SPECIAL DIRECTION NOTE: If you do go to Dark Hollow Falls, be sure to come back down to the Rose River Fire Road to head back 1.1 miles to Fishers Gap Overlook and your car. There is another trail up by Dark Hollow Falls that leads to Skyline Drive, but it will take you nowhere near your car!!!

CONGRATULATIONS!

You have just completed a
SHENANDOAH NATIONAL PARK
SCAVENGER HIKE ADVENTURE!

Rose River Falls Loop to Rose River Falls & Dark Hollow Falls

10 Points for Each Item Found
TOTAL SCORE: _____
CERTIFIED ACHIEVEMENT LEVEL: _____

over **50** to **100** points: **City Slicker**
over **100** to **150** points: **Pioneer Scout**
over **150** points: **Frontier Explorer**

Name(s): _____

Witness(es) thereof: _____

_____

Date: _____

10
Scavenger Hike Adventure

MODERATE

2.2 MILES ROUNDTRIP

2 HOURS

Compton Peak

Why This is a Great Trail! This Scavenger Hike Adventure leads you to the peak of beautiful **Compton Mountain** at an elevation of **2,909 feet**! You will begin your hike on the *famous* **Appalachian Trail (AT),** one of the longest hiking trails on planet earth! It runs from Georgia all the way to Maine, about **2,175 miles**! You will find **incredible views** from the peak of the mountain! You will search for **witches in the woods**, a hidden **metal marker in the forest,** a **boulder as big as a house,** and **amazing white splotches** on trees. You will find the **food that George Washington fed his men** that tastes like a bitter combination of licorice and tapioca! This Scavenger Hike Adventure will definitely make you hungry for more hikes!

Where's the Trail? This trail is in the North District of Shenandoah National Park at **mile 10.4** on the Skyline Drive. Compton Gap Trailhead is across the Skyline Drive from the Compton Gap parking lot. Look for the white blaze on a tree to know you are on the Appalachian Trail.

About the Trail: This is a **MODERATE** trail that probably will not have a lot of hikers on it. It is a gradual climb most of the way to Compton Peak. There are a couple of steep and very rocky sections on this hike!

REMEMBER . . . ROCKS CAN BE VERY SLIPPERY WHEN WET.

How Long is This Hike? This Scavenger Hike Adventure is about **2.2 miles roundtrip** and you should allow about **2 hours** or so.

Things To Hunt For

(Earn 10 points for each treasure you find.)

①

Find Fantastic Ferns in the Forest!

(At the very beginning of the trail---on both sides of the trail)
SPECIAL HINT: Be sure you crossed the Skyline Drive before you start searching for the ferns! These *fantastic* ferns are a *fantastic* way to start a *fantastic* hike! There are about **60 different kinds of ferns** in the park! Ferns grow in both moist and dry spots in Shenandoah National Park! Beautiful!

10 POINTS

②

Find Many Many Fallen Trees!

(On the left and right of the trail)
SPECIAL HINT: You just might be thinking . . . why are there so many fallen trees in Shenandoah National Park? If you come in early spring you will see all the broken tree limbs and downed trees that the **harsh winter ice storms** have left! **Hurricanes, landslides, high winds, and insects** also bring down trees here in the park. Don't worry! Be happy! The forest always grows back and it is exciting to watch the new plants head to the sky!

10 POINTS

❸

Find a Boulder as Big as a House!

10 POINTS

(On the left of the trail---you cannot miss it.)
SPECIAL HINT: Wow! What a rock! This boulder is **greenstone**, the most common rock in Shenandoah National Park! It looks grayish on the outside because rain, wind, and ice have worn the green color away! On the inside it is still green! It was once **black lava rock**! This boulder is over 550 million years old! This whole area was once covered by lava. Hot . . . hot . . . hot!!!

❹

Find Lots of White Splotches on the Same Boulder on #3!

10 POINTS

(You are standing by it.)
SPECIAL HINT: You are looking at **lichen (pronounced LIKE-in).** This lichen looks as if it is just sitting on the rock doing nothing! Wrong! This lichen is alive and it is a combination of **fungus and algae** and is incredible! It will live thousands of years and acid in the lichen will eventually break this rock down into tiny pieces that will become soil! Those white "splotches" are really pretty amazing!

LICHEN AND ALL PLANTS AND ANIMALS IN SHENANDOAH NATIONAL PARK ARE PROTECTED. PLEASE DO NOT HARM ANY PLANT OR LICHEN.

❺

Find the Squirrel Snack that George Washington Once Fed to His Men!

10 POINTS

(Count 62 steps past the boulder in #4---look on the rocks.)
SPECIAL HINT: **Rock tripe** looks like *crumpled dead leaves.* Believe it or not . . . this is another kind of **lichen**! It is edible when boiled, but tastes like a combination of bitter licorice and tapioca and sometimes creates stomach problems. Ugh! **George Washington** ran out of food at Valley Forge and had rock tripe boiled for his men. **Flying squirrels** enjoy this snack. That is one of several differences between a flying squirrel and you!

PLEASE DO NOT EAT THE ROCK TRIPE. ALL LIVING THINGS ARE PROTECTED IN THIS NATIONAL PARK. YOU MAY, HOWEVER, EAT BERRIES OR OTHER FRUIT WHILE YOU ARE IN THE PARK.

6

Find Green Designs on a Tree!

10 POINTS

(Count 18 steps past the boulder with rock tripe---look on the left of the trail.)
SPECIAL HINT: Yes! You've found it once again! Lichen!
There are **thousands of different kinds of lichen.** This one looks like light green flaking paint! Lichen comes in many different colors! We hope you are likin' finding lichen!

7

Find the Rock Steps!

10 POINTS

(Near lots of broken and cracked rocks)
SPECIAL HINT: You are looking at **zillions of rocks** that are here because of water **freezing and thawing** on the mountains! Water gets into cracks in the rocks and when it freezes the water expands as it turns into ice. This thawing and freezing over and over again eventually breaks the rocks and they roll on down the mountain.

8

Find a Giant Huggable Old Oak Tree!

10 POINTS

(Right before the trail makes a sharp left turn and starts to climb ---on the right)
SPECIAL HINT: If you didn't notice the curve in the trail, you will practically walk right into this tree! **Oaks** are **one of the most common trees** in Shenandoah National Park. This tree is a good one to hug because it helps you realize how humongous it is! If you haven't hugged a tree yet today, here is your chance! If you do . . . you will officially be a tree hugger!

9

Find the Nursing Tree!

10 POINTS

(On the left of the giant oak tree you just hugged---on the right of the trail)
SPECIAL HINT: Look for a **live tree growing out of the large twisted dead stump**! Just like a mother gives nourishment to a baby, this dead stump . . . believe it or not . . . is giving nourishment to this tree! Often, dead trees and stumps provide life for new things to live and grow! They are called "**nursing trees.**"

10

Find Lots of Witches in the Woods!

10 POINTS

(Count 45 steps from the old oak tree--- look on the right of the trail---growing in clumps.)
SPECIAL HINT: There are lots of trees of the same kind growing close together in **clumps** on the right side of the trail. The leaves are oval and wavy and toothed on the edges. These are **witch hazel** trees!

These trees are very crafty! They will bloom **yellow spidery flowers** in the fall around Halloween time *usually after all of their leaves have fallen off.* The seed pods explode, sending seeds as far as 20 feet away! That's why these witches in the woods grow in clumps. You will find many more of these trees along the trail. You can find one at **the top of Compton Peak**! There is even a magical potion in the bark that people use to heal their skin (**witch hazel oil**)! This is one magical tree!

11

Find a Round Metal Marker!

10 POINTS

(On the right of the trail---just off the trail---after humongous rocks on the right---40 steps past a log water bar---on a concrete post)
SPECIAL HINT: Find this very official marker from the **United States Department of the Interior.**

⑫ Find an Amazing Tree Growing Right out of a Rock!

10 POINTS

(Hike a while---on the right of the trail---after a sharp right turn---behind a twisted dead tree that is on the ground---almost touching the trail.)
SPECIAL HINT: Trees in Shenandoah National Park must learn to deal with rocks so they can continue growing in the rocky **Appalachian Mountains**! You will notice many tree roots here in the park that break right through rocks to continue their search for water and food! This tree is an interesting sight here in the mountains!

PUT YOUR BOOK AWAY UNTIL YOU REACH THE MARKER FOR COMPTON PEAK!

FOLLOW THE BLUE BLAZES AND DEFINITELY WATCH YOUR STEP!

⑬ Find the Concrete Trail Marker for Compton Peak!

10 POINTS

(You can't miss it!)
SPECIAL HINT: Take the side trail to your right! Head to the top of **Compton Mountain** for a view that will blow you away! Follow the blue blazes to get to the peak!

⑭ Find the Summit of Compton Mountain!

10 POINTS

(At the top)
SPECIAL HINT: Take a load off when you reach the top and enjoy the views from **Compton Peak**! Look around and feel the awesomeness and peacefulness of being among the trees, rocks, and mountain peaks in Shenandoah National Park! Ahhhhh.

⑮

Find the Miniature Oak Trees!

___

10 POINTS

(On the top of the mountain)
SPECIAL HINT: You are now at **2,909 feet elevation!** Hey! What happened to those huge, tall old oak trees? The **weather is cold and harsh up here** during the winter, **so the trees grow smaller** to stay **closer to the ground** where it is **warmer**! Smart trees!

WALK CAREFULLY DOWN THE ROCKY SLOPES BACK TO SKYLINE DRIVE!

FOLLOW THE TRAIL MARKERS AND BLAZES DOWN THE MOUNTAIN. TAKE THE APPALACHIAN TRAIL NORTH TO THE PARKING LOT!

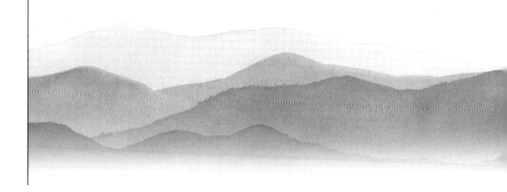

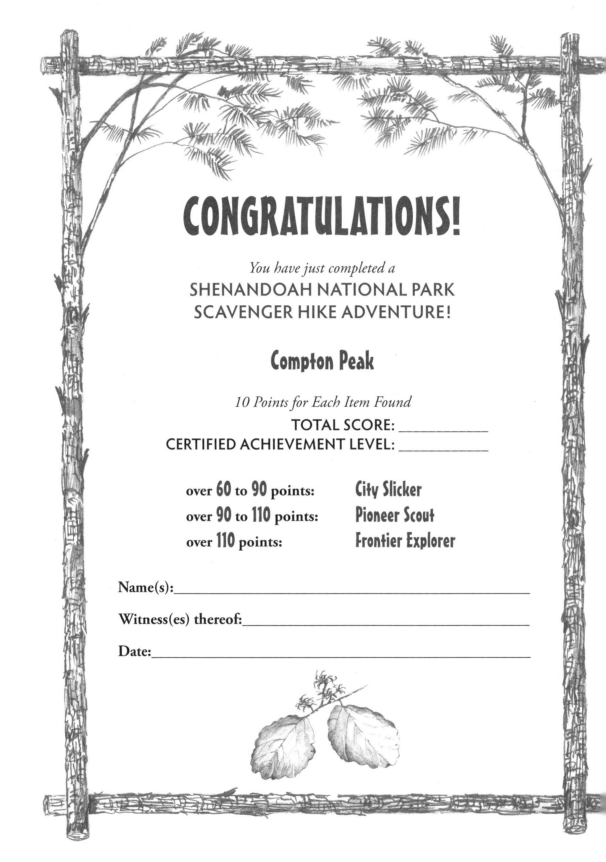

CONGRATULATIONS!

You have just completed a
SHENANDOAH NATIONAL PARK
SCAVENGER HIKE ADVENTURE!

Compton Peak

10 Points for Each Item Found
TOTAL SCORE: _____
CERTIFIED ACHIEVEMENT LEVEL: _____

over **60** to **90** points: **City Slicker**

over **90** to **110** points: **Pioneer Scout**

over **110** points: **Frontier Explorer**

Name(s):_____

Witness(es) thereof:_____

Date:_____

11
Scavenger Hike Adventure

EXTREME

4.9 MILE LOOP

4-5 HOURS

Sugarloaf Loop

Why This is a Great Trail! This Scavenger Hike Adventure is like **4 incredible adventures in one!** You will **hike along a narrow path** and feel much like the Indians did when they first explored this area thousands of years ago! You will discover an awesome **mountain laurel jungle**, an **old fire road** with zillions of flowers, and **awesome mountain views** that will make your eyes bug out! Whew! What a hike! You will find some really unusual treasures like a **stone throne**, an unusual **stone bear head**, a **deer head up in a tree**, a **toothpick forest,** and a tree that has a **trunk that looks like bubble wrap**! Find the launching pad where pilots take their **hang gliders** and jump off a cliff and soar in the sky! You will even find a **rope that looks like it's growing out of a tree!** You will **be amazed!!!** Go ahead and pack a camera for this adventure, but you won't need it! You will never forget Sugarloaf Loop!

Where's the Trail? The trailhead is located just south of Hogback Overlook on the east side of the Skyline Drive at **milepost 21** in the North District of the park. There is parking for about 10 cars at a hidden turn on the west side of Skyline Drive. There are 2 boulders at the south end of the parking lot that you will pass between to get on the Appalachian Trail. Turn left on the AT and walk across the Skyline Drive. Continue north on the AT.

About the Trail: This **EXTREME** Scavenger Hike Adventure has a wide variety of trail conditions that change every mile or so! The fire road trail section is open to the sun and could be quite hot in the summer. This trail is uphill, downhill, level, shaded, narrow, wide, rocky, sunny, and has steep switchbacks. You name it, this trail's got it!

How Long is This Hike? This Scavenger Hike Adventure is a **4.9-mile loop** and will take your exploration party about **4-5 hours** or so! Start early in the morning especially in the summer and pack a big lunch, lots of water, and a few delicious snacks! You will probably want something a little more than just peanuts and raisins! Pack a hearty snack for a hearty hike!!!

Things To Hunt For
(Earn 10 points for each treasure you find.)

❶ Find the Starting Point for this Adventure!

10 POINTS

(Go to the south end of the parking area---go left on the trail at the edge of the parking lot---cross Skyline Drive---continue heading north on the AT.) SPECIAL HINT: You will hike on the famous **Appalachian Trail** for a little more than 1/4-mile before coming to the Sugarloaf Trail intersection. The Appalachian Trail runs from Georgia to Maine for a total distance of about **2,175 miles**!

After this section you will have hiked the entire AT *except for about 2,174.7 miles!*

❷ Find Zillions of Ferns!

10 POINTS

(On both sides of the trail---a humongous field of ferns) SPECIAL HINT: It is obvious that ferns totally absolutely love this spot! The "leaves" on a fern are actually called "**fronds**." The fronds help capture sunlight, water, and nutrients. That's what fronds are for!

❸
Find the Giant Stone Bear Head in the Woods!

10 POINTS

(Start looking right away---soon after you see the ferns---on the right---as you start up the hill.)
SPECIAL HINT: Use your imagination! This large boulder surrounded by ferns looks like the **head of a bear looking away from the trail into the woods.** Look for the face, ears, and muzzle (nose) of the bear. If you *bearly* pass it, you will *bearly* miss it because it will then look like an ordinary boulder.

❹
Find the Giant Stone Throne!

10 POINTS

(At the top of the hill---on the right)
SPECIAL HINT: You just won't be able to pass this throne without sitting on it! It looks like a **giant stone chair** for a giant king of the forest! You will certainly not confuse the *stone throne* with a *thrown stone.* This is **definitely photo time** for anyone claiming King of the Mountain status!

❺
Find a Deer Eating a Big Chunk of Wood!

10 POINTS

(Count 50 steps past the throne---on the right---straight ahead---push your chin up 1 inch.)

SPECIAL HINT: This tree looks exactly like a deer chewing on a big chunk of wood. You'll know you found it when you say, "Oh my gosh, it does look just like a giant deer eating a big chunk of wood!"

6

Find Sugar-loaf Trail!

_____
10 POINTS

(Concrete marker---on the left of the trail)
SPECIAL HINT: You will now leave the **Appalachian Trail** and turn right to follow the narrow path down **Sugarloaf Trail**. How many miles is it to **Pole Bridge Link**?

7

Find the Jungle of Mountain Laurel!

_____
10 POINTS

(Up ahead a bit---on both sides of the trail---as you go down the lo-o-o-o-ng hill)
SPECIAL HINT: **Mountain laurel** has short, thick, leathery, kind of shiny (very shiny when wet) dark green leaves about as long as your finger. In the spring this jungle blooms with thousands of **beautiful pink-and-white flowers**. Can you just imagine? It would be like walking through the middle of a bouquet of flowers! Awesome! You will hike for quite a while (seriously) through this "jungle."

8

Find the "Green Carpet" Lining the Trail!

_____
10 POINTS

(On the edge of the trail ---on both sides---as you continue down this long hill)
SPECIAL HINT: Look for low-growing soft green **moss**. It looks like velvety carpet. **Moss** never has a flower and moss never makes any seeds. If anyone in your group knows how it spreads to create new moss . . . give yourself 10 bonus points. Ask a ranger to learn about sp _ _ _s.

REMEMBER TO NEVER PICK OR HARM ANY PLANT IN SHENANDOAH NATIONAL PARK. EVERY SINGLE PLANT IS PROTECTED.

❾ Find Where "X's" Mark the Spot!

(Hike quite a while---look on a log completely crossing the trail---just keep going---you can't miss it!)

SPECIAL HINT: You will hike quite a long while before you get to this log. Someone will probably say, "Do you think we passed it?" A log will completely cross the trail and it will be marked with **"X's."** Why did a ranger or trail volunteer carve those "X's" in the log? To give your hiking boots a better grip!

10 POINTS | **WET WOOD IS VERY SLIPPERY.**

❿ Find a Double Blue Blaze!

(On the left of the trail---just before a turn in the trail)
 SPECIAL HINT:
The *double* blue blaze (rectangle) painted on a tree means there is a **turn up ahead**.

10 POINTS

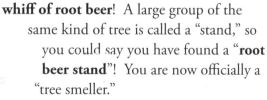

⓫ Find a Very Smelly Tree!

(Hike a while---look for skinny trees that are like toothpicks---on both sides of the trail.)

SPECIAL HINT: The bark has horizontal raised lines and the leaves are sawtoothed and oval. These skinny trees are **black birch** and if you gently scratch a thin branch you will get a huge **whiff of root beer**! A large group of the same kind of tree is called a "stand," so you could say you have found a "**root beer stand**"! You are now officially a "tree smeller."

10 POINTS

⑫

Find a Witch Named Hazel!

(Shortish trees growing in clumps---ovalish/almost roundish leaves with wavy edges---on both sides of the trail---lots of 'em)
SPECIAL HINT:

A. These witch hazel trees bloom a **spidery yellow flower** around Halloween *after* all the leaves have dropped off.

B. If you rub your bare arm on the bark it **might make your skin tingle**.

C. The tree's **seeds explode** and travel as far as **20 feet**.

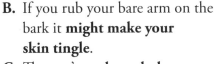

D. At midnight the trees join branches and form a large circle. A strange humming sound can be heard echoing throughout these mountains.

E. **Witch hazel oil** is found in **skin care products** sold at your local drugstore.

10 POINTS

Only **one** of A, B, C, D or E **is untrue.** Untrue:_____

⑬

Find a "Bubble-Wrapped" Tree!

10 POINTS

(Count 2 steps after the stream bed---on the left of the trail.)
SPECIAL HINT: This tree has **very interesting** and **unusual bark**. It looks like brown bubble wrap. It is just about 2 steps to the left of the trail.

⑭

Find the Sign of Early Settlers!

10 POINTS

(Count 20 steps past the bubble-wrapped tree---on the left and right of the trail.)
SPECIAL HINT: Can you tell these were once **rock walls**? Early pioneers lived in this area. Pioneers would stack up rocks and build walls as they cleared the land for farming.

⑮
Find a Possible Bear Den!

10 POINTS

(On the left---look 40 steps off the trail into the woods---just before the next trail intersection---stay on the trail.)
SPECIAL HINT: This giant group of **greenstone** boulders has openings where a bear could **den** in the winter. There are about **300-500 black bears in Shenandoah National Park**. Bears den in trees, small rock openings, and caves. Black bears in Shenandoah do not actually hibernate, but they do take long, very deep naps. They can be up and about any day of the year . . . including right now!

IF YOU EVER SEE A BEAR . . . GIVE IT SPACE. DO NOT APPROACH IT. BEARS CAN RUN 30 MILES PER HOUR AND OLD TIMERS SAY THEY CAN CLIMB A TREE FASTER THAN YOU COULD FALL OUT OF A TREE! DON'T EVER RUN FROM A BEAR. DON'T EVER TURN YOUR BACK ON A BEAR.

⑯
Find Pole Bridge Link Trail

10 POINTS

(Find the concrete marker---at the trail intersection.)
SPECIAL HINT:
Go LEFT on Pole Bridge Link Trail.

⑰
Find Bear Scat!

10 POINTS

(Look all along the trail---as you continue to look---go on to clue #18.)
SPECIAL HINT: **Bear scat** (droppings) is easily identifiable because you can closely examine the pile and see the berries or whatever the bear was eating. Bear scat is brown or black and tapered or flat at the ends. It sometimes has a sweet smell. There are about **1 to 2 bears for every square mile** in this national park. This entire adventure today is about a 5-mile loop. Sooooooo . . . give yourself 10 bonus points for each bear you see on the trail. If you have already found bear scat . . . give yourself the points!
NEVER TOUCH BEAR SCAT WITH YOUR FINGERS. ALWAYS USE A STICK TO CHECK IT OUT.

⑱

Find Green Lichen (Pronounced Like-In)!

_____

10 POINTS

(On the left of the trail---on a boulder) SPECIAL HINT: This green **lichen** is growing on a boulder about the size of a 3-person pup tent. It looks like flaking light-green paint. **Lichen** is a combination of **fungus** and **algae** and can live for thousands of years. The acid in the lichen will gradually eat away at this boulder and turn it into soil.

⑲

Find a Pile of Rocks!

_____

10 POINTS

(On the left---right before a tree with a double blue blaze and a fire road) SPECIAL HINT: Someone long ago stacked these rocks perhaps to clear a place for a garden. There were about 450 families living within the boundaries of **Shenandoah National Park** before it became a park in **1935**. **President Franklin D. Roosevelt** made the decision that all of those families had to leave their homes and find somewhere else to live. It was quite sad for many of those mountain folks. This park was **one of the first national parks in the eastern United States.**

⑳

Find the Piece of Rope "Growing" out of a Tree!

_____

10 POINTS

(Sit on a log on the right side of the open area---at the next trail junction---look across the opening---while sitting on the log.) SPECIAL HINT: Years ago someone tied this rope around the tree. As the years passed the tree grew around the rope. It now looks like   the rope is _growing_ out of the tree. Amazing! This is a great time for a break!

At the 4-way trail junction be sure to take the Keyser Run Road heading 1 mile back to Skyline Drive. Notice the yellow blazes. This is also a horse trail.

NOW . . . PUT THE BOOK AWAY AND ENJOY A 1-MILE AWESOME WILDFLOWER PILGRIMAGE IN THE SPRING AND SUMMER. AN INCREDIBLE VARIETY OF FLOWERS AND PLANTS BORDER THE ROAD ALL THE WAY TO THE SKYLINE DRIVE. IT IS A GENTLE UPWARD SLOPE. OCCASIONALLY . . . "STOP AND SMELL THE FLOWERS."

㉑

Find the Appalachian Trail!

10 POINTS

(Cross the yellow-chained gate---then cross the Skyline Drive---hike the length of one football field (100 yards)---to the Appalachian Trail.)

SPECIAL HINT: Go left **(south)** on the AT. Follow the white blazes on the trees that mean you are on the **Appalachian Trail**. Thru-hikers are hikers who will travel the entire AT from Georgia to Maine (2,175 miles). It takes about 6 months to do that. **Thru-hikers** get to know each other along the trail and most of them have **trail names**. Here are a few examples of actual thru-hiker nicknames: A tall person from Poland, **Hiking Pole;** a hiker from Kentucky, **Bluegrass**; and a bald-headed hiker who ate lots of graham crackers and icing along the trail was named **Gingerbread Man**. Thru-hikers are usually given their names by fellow hikers. Go ahead and give someone in your group a trail nickname.

22
Find the View at the Top!

10 POINTS

(At the top of this hill---where the AT takes a left turn ---the viewing boulder is on the right of the trail.)
SPECIAL HINT: Take a break! Trust us! You need to be rested for the next section. At the viewpoint you will find a group of boulders. A large piece of a **greenstone** boulder is chipped off one of them and you can see a great example of why it is called "greenstone." It is dark green inside the boulder and weathered gray on the outside. Enjoy the view . . . and rest. (See next clue.)

BE SURE TO CONTINUE FOLLOWING THE AT SOUTH.

23
Find the Broken Escalator!

10 POINTS

(Up, up, and away)
SPECIAL HINT: Just kidding! This is actually a rock step trail going up. Do you wish it was a real and working escalator? This is the steepest section of the trail. There are 100 **switchbacks** to get to the top . . . NOT!!! There are only about 10. Take it easy! Don't push it! Good News! There is likely a breeze waiting for you at the top of this ridge!

24
Find the Buck Head!

10 POINTS

(Straight in front of you---at a right turn switchback)
SPECIAL HINT: You must stop and look at this a while. The tree looks like a giant deer with antlers! A tree that looks like a buck is enough to force a rest break. Take 5 . . . You're welcome! You're doin' great! The view ahead is incredible and is really worth the climb!

㉕

Find the Spot Where People Strap a Contraption to Their Backs & Jump off a Cliff (Hang Glide)!

_____
10 POINTS

(Hike a while! Find the concrete trail marker---you can't miss it--- it says, "100 yards to launch site.")
SPECIAL HINT: **Stay on the AT.** This big flat grassy area is the launching pad for **hang gliders**! You strap this colorful gigantic contraption on your back and simply jump off the cliff! You might want to add that activity to your list for later today.

DON'T FORGET TO GET A PERMIT BEFORE YOU HANG GLIDE.

㉖

Find Your Car!

_____
10 POINTS

(Cross the Skyline Drive and follow the AT South.)
SPECIAL HINT: You have almost made it! Just stay on the world-famous Appalachian Trail until you see your car. You may recognize a few things because earlier today you walked a little part of this trail. Trust us . . . you will twist and turn a bit on this trail but you will get there! **Be sure to stay on the AT----don't turn left on Sugarloaf Trail by the concrete marker.** Go ahead and give yourself 5 extra points when you actually touch your car! Have you ever been as excited to see a parking lot? Congratulations!!!

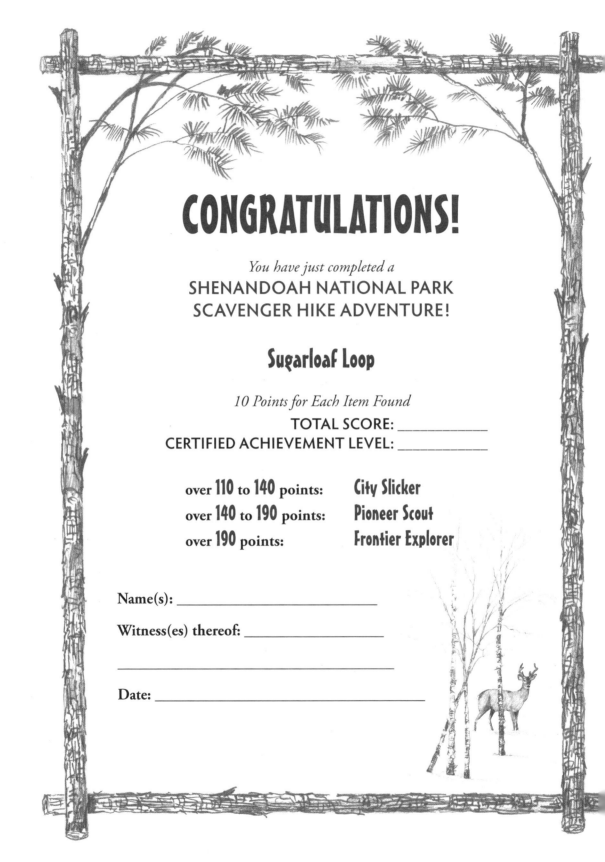

CONGRATULATIONS!

You have just completed a

SHENANDOAH NATIONAL PARK
SCAVENGER HIKE ADVENTURE!

Sugarloaf Loop

10 Points for Each Item Found

TOTAL SCORE: _____

CERTIFIED ACHIEVEMENT LEVEL: _____

over **110** to **140** points: **City Slicker**

over **140** to **190** points: **Pioneer Scout**

over **190** points: **Frontier Explorer**

Name(s): _____

Witness(es) thereof: _____

_____

Date: _____

Fri april 2021 (handwritten)

12
Scavenger Hike Adventure

EASY

1 MILE LONG

ABOUT 1 HOUR

"...much less interesting North section" (handwritten, left margin)

Prefer Thornton Gap & South for views (handwritten, left margin)

Fox Hollow Trail

Why This is a Great Trail! This awesome Scavenger Hike Adventure is a journey of a different kind! Crank your time machine back over 150 years to **1856** and strap yourself in! That was the year when **Thomas and Martha Fox** bought a farm right here in **Fox Hollow**! It is also the same year that **Abe Lincoln** gave 50 speeches trying to help John Fremont become president of the United States and an article in a newspaper explained the "dangers" of *hoop skirts* on a windy day!

Journey back in time and find the **old rusty wire** from farm fences and giant **rock piles** stacked high by the Foxes to clear the land for planting crops. Find **humongous tulip trees** and **grapevines** gone wild! Sit in the very same **giant sycamore tree** that once stood as the only tree on the hill. Find a **very special gravestone** and a **shiny plant** that settlers used in cemeteries. The Fox family lived here for 5 generations! Welcome back . . . in time . . . to Fox Hollow!

Where's the Trail? The trailhead is located right across the Skyline Drive from Dickey Ridge Visitor Center at **mile 4.6** in the North District of the national park. Park in the lot for the visitor center on the west side of the Skyline Drive. **Start your Scavenger Hike Adventure by stopping in at the visitor center.**

About the Trail: This EASY loop trail is level, shaded, and is do-able for all ages. It used to be an old road that the Fox family used to travel to the city of Front Royal to get supplies.

How Long is This Hike? This Scavenger Hike Adventure is a 1-mile loop and will take your exploration party about an hour or so!

Things To Hunt For

(Earn 10 points for each treasure you find.)

(You might find some of these critters along the trail . . .)

1

Find These Awesome Critters!

Black Bear
Baby Fawn
Monarch Butterfly
Eastern Screech Owl
Chipmunk
Groundhog
Eastern Box Turtle
Racoon
Grouse
Brook Trout
Hawk

SPECIAL HINT: You will be sure to find all of them in the **Dickey Ridge Visitor Center**! It is a great place! Don't miss the **10-minute movie** about beautiful **Shenandoah National Park**!

10 POINTS

2

Find the Flagpole!

10 POINTS

(Behind the visitor center)
SPECIAL HINT: This tall flagpole can't be missed. It is near a grassy path.

3

Find the Weed that Says, "Got Milk?"!

(Look on the right and left of the grassy path---near the flagpole.)
SPECIAL HINT:
Milkweed grows about 2-to-5 feet tall in sunny areas and has beautiful **pink flowers in summer** that are butterfly magnets! The plant has a milky white sap inside, so that is why it is called "milkweed." **Monarch butterflies** go wacky over the milkweed flower (it's the only thing they eat) before they

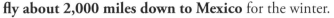

fly about 2,000 miles down to Mexico for the winter. Monarch butterflies lay their eggs on the underside of the milkweed leaves and the caterpillars munch like crazy on the leaves as soon as they are hatched. Eating the milkweed leaves makes the caterpillars and the butterflies they will become . . . incredibly *bad-tasting* for birds . . . so birds will leave them alone. It is no wonder you can listen to the tiny little voice of a monarch butterfly saying, "Got Milk?" . . . Not!!!

REMEMBER TO NEVER EVER PICK PLANTS OR FLOWERS. EVERY SINGLE ONE IS PROTECTED IN SHENANDOAH NATIONAL PARK.

10 POINTS

4

Find Dickey Ridge Trailhead Sign!

10 POINTS

(Cross Skyline Drive.)
SPECIAL HINT: Don't start hiking until you do clue #5. You will go left on **Dickey Ridge Trail** as you begin the loop for **Fox Hollow Trail**. You will be looking down into Fox Hollow as you begin this Scavenger Hike Adventure.

5

Find a Humongous Tulip Tree!

10 POINTS

(Count 65 steps past the trailhead sign---look on the left.)
SPECIAL HINT: There is a pine tree to the left of this awesome tree! Many pioneer cabins were made out of **yellow poplar trees** (also called **tulip trees**). The leaves of a tulip tree look something like a tulip flower. Sometimes tulip trees were so big that it would only **take 1 tree to build an entire cabin!** Thomas Fox and his wife, Martha, lived here in Fox Hollow over 150 years ago. Thomas built a **7-room log house** for his family. Wow!

❻ Find the Grapevines Gone Wild!

I find grapevines winding into trees over branches

10 POINTS

(On the left and right--- everywhere)
SPECIAL HINT: These thick, twisted, brown **grapevines** are growing up, down, sideways, upways, downways, and every whichaways. Thomas and Martha had a **large garden** including a section for grapes. There are so many grapevines on this trail that you can officially say, "I heard it through the grapevine."

❼ Find the Sign that Welcomes You to Fox Hollow Trail!

10 POINTS

(At the next trail marker---at a trail intersection---turn right.)
SPECIAL HINT: Turn right to continue on Fox Hollow Trail. You are walking in the very same steps as **Thomas and Martha Fox**! **Five generations of Foxes** lived here. That means Thomas and Martha and their children, grandchildren, *great*-grandchildren, and *great-great*-grandchildren all lived in Fox Hollow! It was a *great* place then and is a *great* place now!

❽ Find the Big Old Cow Pasture!

10 POINTS

(Count 100 steps from the Fox Hollow trail sign---look all around you.)
SPECIAL HINT: This was once a wide **open pasture** for farm animals! In **1856** Thomas Fox **bought his 450 acres of land** for about $5,000. He had a herd of about **100 cattle**. He also had horses and sheep that may have grazed here in this pasture.
Now . . . mooove along!

at least 10 rock piles ✓

9

Find an Awesome Rock Pile!

10 POINTS

(On the right---you can't miss it.)
SPECIAL HINT: What makes a **rock pile** a*wesome*?
Generations of Foxes added to this rock pile to help keep the
farmland clear for growing crops. This rock pile is **over 150 years
old**, it is humongous, it is historical, and it shows the hard work
required to clear this land for farming. That's why it is *awesome*!

10

Find Some Seasoning for Groundhog or Possum Stew!

10 POINTS

(Directly across from the awesome rock pile---scratch and sniff!)
SPECIAL HINT: If you carefully scratch a **spicebush** branch
with your fingernail, you will
smell the spice. The
spicebush can grow to
about the height of 2 to
3 people sitting on each
other's shoulders. It has
thin branches with kind of
oval leaves, yellow flowers in
the spring, and red berries
in the fall. Pioneers used
it to brew **tea** and also
to **season opossum and
groundhog** meat. "Just a tad
more spicebush seasoning on that
groundhog, please."

11

Find Another Awesome Rock Pile!

10 POINTS

(Up ahead)
SPECIAL HINT: It is believed by many scientists that the
Appalachian Mountains used to be 3 times higher than they
are today and maybe even as high as the **Himalayas**! The rocks
broke off the tops of the peaks and gradually the mountains
were reduced in size. Water gets in the cracks of rocks and
freezes (expands) and then thaws. After that happens over many
years the rocks finally crack and break apart and roll down the
mountain. Amazing!

interesting

12

Find the Fox Family Cemetery!

_____
10 POINTS

(On the left of the trail---behind the rock wall)
SPECIAL HINT:
Many generations of Foxes are buried here, but most of the gravestones are gone.

13

Find the Final Resting Place of Lemuel F. Fox!

_____
10 POINTS

(Biggest gravestone)
SPECIAL HINT: Lemuel was one of Thomas's 3 sons.
Lemuel and his 2 brothers fought for the Confederacy during the Civil War. One brother died of typhoid fever, another died in a battle, and only Lemuel survived to return to the farm. His gravestone reads, "Gone and not forgotten by his daughter."

14

Find the Special Shiny Green Cemetery Plant!

_____
10 POINTS

(On the ground---in the cemetery)
SPECIAL HINT: Look for a vine with **shiny green leaves** growing close to the ground. It has a **blueish-purple flower in the spring**. **Periwinkle** was planted in pioneer cemeteries because it would spread along the ground and no one had to trim it. It is a very pretty plant.

Yes

15

Find the Springbox!

large hand to miss)

10 POINTS

(Cement box---on the right of the trail)
SPECIAL HINT: The national park built this **springbox** after all of the Foxes had moved out of Fox Hollow so this area could be part of Shenandoah National Park. The springbox was used as a water supply source for the dining hall at Dickey Ridge Lodge. **Dickey Ridge Lodge** later became the Dickey Ridge Visitor Center. My, how things do change!

16
Find the Millstone!

10 POINTS

(Count 114 steps from the springbox---look all around---on the right---about 10 feet off the trail.)
SPECIAL HINT: A **millstone** is round and is about the size of a bicycle wheel. It is made out of stone and has a hole in the center. Two millstones would lie up against each other in a mill and a waterwheel would turn the stone to **grind corn** into cornmeal. Cornbread and beans . . . a great country meal! This stone was just a decoration for the farm . . . there were no mills along this stream.

17
Find the Site of an Old Barn!

10 POINTS

(Count 25 steps from the millstone---on the left---across from a tree with a blue blaze.)
SPECIAL HINT: **Edgar Merchant** had a barn at this spot. A short bit of this trail is actually on what was once Edgar's property. He was a neighbor of the Foxes. The barn foundation is under a thick group of spice bushes and other plants.

PLEASE STAY ON THE TRAIL.

18
Find the Double Blue Blaze!

10 POINTS

(On a tree on the left of the trail--- just before a turn in the trail)
SPECIAL HINT: The double blaze (rectangle) painted on the tree alerts hikers that **a "turn" in the trail** is just up ahead.

BE CAREFUL IN THIS ROCKY AREA.

19
Find the Old Rusty Wire Fence!

10 POINTS

(On the left---next to the trail---on top of rocks)
SPECIAL HINT: This **wire fence** goes on and on and was built to **separate the farm from the road**. You are actually hiking on an old road that used to lead to the city of **Front Royal**. Picture cows in the field, crops growing, a barn just behind you, and a shiny wire fence lining the road as you ride your horse on up to Front Royal to purchase some licorice from the general store.

⓴

Find Where a Windmill Used To Be!

10 POINTS

(Hike a while---after a sharp left turn in the trail---hike a bit more---on the left.)

SPECIAL HINT: You are searching for a **sycamore tree** with 3 giant branches. Lemuel, Jr., said that he once installed a windmill in this tree! This beautiful sycamore tree used to stand all alone on this hill so it was easy for the windmill to try and catch the wind!

㉑

Find a Giant Twin-Trunked Tree!

10 POINTS

(Hike a while--- look on the left---in the woods.)

SPECIAL HINT: Find a tree that looks more like a "twin" tree. It has **2 trunks**. Young trees are sometimes struck by lightning, gnawed by an animal, or injured by the wind. Those natural events can cause the tree to split into 2 trunks. **Shenandoah National Park was established in 1935** and trees and plants have been growing wild here ever since. This is another giant tulip tree!

㉒

Find a Giant Triplet-Trunked Tree!

10 POINTS

(On the right---blue painted rectangle on this tree)

SPECIAL HINT: You just found a twin-trunked tree and are searching for a triplet-trunked tree. Yes, you guessed it. It has 3 trunks. In fact, it is a triplet-trunked **tulip tree** . . . truly!

㉓

Find Holes Made by One of the Largest Woodpeckers on Planet Earth!

10 POINTS

(Count 55 steps from the triplet tree---look around on trees---on the left.)

SPECIAL HINT: The **pileated (pronounced Pile-ee-ated or Pill-ee-ated . . . it's up to you) woodpecker** has a red crest, a black body, and looks a lot like the old cartoon character Woody Woodpecker! It makes **large oval holes** and is the second largest woodpecker in North America!

㉔
Find a White-Tailed Deer!

10 POINTS

(All along the trail)

SPECIAL HINT: If you haven't yet noticed, there are *many, many* **white-tailed deer** in Shenandoah National Park! Deer like to nibble on grass and plants around the **edges** of forests. That is why you just might see 1 . . . 2 . . . 3 . . . or more along the Skyline Drive! If you have already seen one on this trail, give yourself the points.

ALWAYS RESPECT THE WILDLIFE IN SHENANDOAH NATIONAL PARK. Give them plenty of space. If they change their behavior when you are watching them . . . you are probably too close. Never feed wildlife! The deer asked us to remind you that the speed limit is 35 m.p.h. on Skyline Drive. They said to pass along their thanks.

NOW . . . ENJOY YOUR WALK BACK TO THE VISITOR CENTER! GO STRAIGHT AT THE CONCRETE POST TO RETURN TO WHERE YOU STARTED. CHECK THE CONCRETE MARKER TO BE SURE YOU ARE HEADING TO THE VISITOR CENTER.

CONGRATULATIONS!

You have just completed a
SHENANDOAH NATIONAL PARK
SCAVENGER HIKE ADVENTURE!

Fox Hollow Trail

10 Points for Each Item Found

TOTAL SCORE: _____

CERTIFIED ACHIEVEMENT LEVEL: _____

over **80** to **100** points: **City Slicker**

over **100** to **170** points: **Pioneer Scout**

over **170** points: **Frontier Explorer**

Name(s): _____

Witness(es) thereof: _____

_____

Date: _____

13
Scavenger Hike Adventure

EASY
2 MILES ROUNDTRIP
1.5 HOURS

Appalachian Trail Ridge Hike

Why This is a Great Trail! This Scavenger Hike Adventure is exactly what you need . . . to see if you are ready for an adventure of a lifetime! This is a **short "sampler"** of the *mighty long Appalachian Trail*! Every year, over 1,000 inspired folks will start out to hike the entire **2,175 miles** of this awesome trail that runs through **14 states from Georgia to Maine.** Notice we said *"start out,"* because only 25% will make it all the way and "git 'er done!" If you enjoy the adventure today, why not block out 6 months on your calendar next year to take a *long . . . very long* walk in the woods!

This short hike on the AT stretches along a ridge **thousands of feet above** the **Shenandoah Valley.** You will peek through the forest and find **towns and villages** down in the valley . . . the valley so low. Find incredible signs of the **largest forest fire** in the history of this national park and **beautiful trees that have helped a ship set sail!** Find a **giant old oak** tree and the **oldest rocks** in the entire national park (about a billion years old)! Be careful . . . you might just get inspired to come back for the other *2,174* miles that are waiting for you! Welcome to the AT!

Where's the Trail? This Scavenger Hike Adventure is totally on the AT and it begins at the south end (far end) of the Pinnacles Picnic Grounds at mile **36.7** in the Central District of the park. Drive all the way through the picnic area past the picnic pavilion. The AT heads into the woods directly to the left as you face the **winter restrooms** (pit toilet with no running water or electricity). Your adventure *begins* where the blacktop ends. *Go south on the AT.*

About the Trail: This is a pretty **EASY** trail. It is sometimes narrow and sometimes quite rocky with a bit of a slope. The picnic grounds is one of the nicest places you will ever find . . . to eat your lunch. "Supersize" your adventure . . . this is a great picnic/hike combo! Talk about "supersize" . . . the picnic pavilion here even has 4 fireplaces! You will be hiking at 3,400 feet elevation.

How Long is This Hike? This Scavenger Hike Adventure is **2.0 miles roundtrip.** You should allow **1 1/2 hours** or a little more for time to take a break on the large flat rock overlooking Old Rag Mountain.

Things To Hunt For

(Earn 10 points for each treasure you find.)

①

Find One Spot Where You Can Spot 3 Stone Water Fountains!

———
10 POINTS

(Count 75 steps to the left of the trail entrance---past the winter restroom (pit toilet)---along a narrow paved path.) SPECIAL HINT: Stand at the stone water fountain and face the picnic shelter. Look all around to find 2 other stone fountains. This entire beautiful picnic area and the fountains were built by President Roosevelt's "**CCC boys**" (**Civilian Conservation Corps**) about 70 years ago. When the economy was really bad Roosevelt created a special program that gave young men jobs. A CCC workers' camp was located behind this water fountain . . . down the hill. You can learn all about the Civilian Conservation Corps at the **Byrd Visitor Center**. There is even a life-size statue of one of the CCC workers called "**Iron Mike**." Don't miss the awesome displays and the movies at this visitor center! Really! Check it out!

②

Find Long Soft Pine Needles Over Your Head!

_____

10 POINTS

(Walk back to the trail. Count 17 steps down the trail---look up!) SPECIAL HINT: This pine tree has the softest, greenest long needles you can imagine! **White pine** trees always have 5 needles in a packet. Go ahead and count . . . 1 . . . 2 . . . 3 . . . 4 . . . 5 . . . Hey! This must be a white pine tree!

③

Find a Tree that Helps a Ship Sail out to Sea!

_____

10 POINTS

(Watch closely---at second left turn in the trail---take the side path on the right---count 15 steps down the side path.) SPECIAL HINT: The tall branches of this tree have been used for **masts on ships**. Pretty cool! Hey, could this possibly be another white pine tree?

④

Find a Sign of the Largest Fire in Park History!

_____

10 POINTS

(Count 100 steps from the side path in clue #3---start looking on the left side of the trail.) SPECIAL HINT: Blackened stumps and trees are still all along the trail from a **fire** that started in the **Pinnacles Picnic Grounds** in the year 2000 and joined up with another fire that started a couple of days later on **Old Rag Mountain.** The fire burned over 24,000 acres. Wow! The forest will eventually hide all signs of the fire, but not yet.

⑤

Find a Giant Old Oak Tree with a "V" for Virginia!

_____

10 POINTS

(Hike a ways---on left of the trail---two branches of a huge oak tree---shaped like a "V"---close to the trail.) SPECIAL HINT: It would take at least 2 hikers with arms outstretched to circle this huge **white oak tree**. Keep your eyes to the left as you go down the hill. This is one of the largest trees on this trail!

6

Find a Giant Tree that Was Toasted by the Big Fire!

(Count 110 steps from the giant old oak tree shaped like a "V" in #5---look around on the left of the trail.)

SPECIAL HINT:

This mighty tree still shows the damage from the **big fire**. As you pass the tree, look on the far side of the tree. Wow!

10 POINTS

7

Find a Thru-Hiker!

(All along the trail---as you go on to #8)

SPECIAL HINT: Many hikers start the **AT** in Georgia in the springtime and hike all the way to Maine. It sometimes takes about 6 months. All **thru-hikers** have "**trail names**" and write messages to each other in books at hiking shelters all along the way. Some recent actual trail names include **Goldilocks**, **Jolly Green**, and **Packrat**. What trail name will you use someday when you do the entire AT? If someone in your group can't think of one---give them one!

10 POINTS

8

Find an Old Telephone Pole with a White Blaze on It!

(On the right of the trail---almost on the trail)

SPECIAL HINT: The **white blaze (rectangle)** painted on the pole tells you this is the Appalachian Trail. The entire **AT** is marked with white blazes on trees and rocks and sometimes even a telephone pole. When was the last year this pole was inspected by a **pole inspector**? You must **answer that question to get the points**.

10 POINTS

9

Find a Boulder Bigger than a Bus!

(On the left of the trail---almost touching the trail---there is a white blaze on the boulder.)

SPECIAL HINT: Enough said!

10 POINTS

10

Find the Dock on Lake Arrowhead!

10 POINTS

(Count 56 steps past the big boulder in #9---look down in the valley.)
SPECIAL HINT: **Lake Arrowhead** has a dam and it catches water from all of the steep mountain hollers around here. The little town of **Luray** gets some of its drinking water from that lake. It is like a giant rain catcher!

11

Find the Town of Luray!

10 POINTS

(Beyond the lake---down below you)
SPECIAL HINT: **Luray (pronounced LOU-ray** by locals) is home to the famous Luray Caverns that are visited by about a half-million people each year. **Thru-hikers** look forward to towns near the AT so they can pick up needed supplies. Sometimes friends or family will mail a **"care package"** to a local post office and the hiker can't wait to stop by and pick it up! A thru-hiker's pack usually weighs about 40 pounds or so!!! Thru-hikers often carry their *houses* (tents) as well as food and other supplies on their backs! What a load!!!

12

Find a Nearly 75-Mile-Long Metal Cable!

10 POINTS

(As you continue and go down the trail---the cable is above the ground---on the trail.)
SPECIAL HINT: An underground telephone cable was buried here by the **CCC boys** and once carried telephone lines from **Front Royal** down to **Simmons Gap** at mile 73.2. It is not used anymore. Find 1 piece of that nearly 75-mile-long cable.
Hello?? Can you hear me now???

⓭

Find Giant Holes Made by One of the Largest Woodpeckers on Planet Earth!

_____

10 POINTS

(Count 38 steps from the end of the metal cable---on the right---just before a tree with a white blaze.)
SPECIAL HINT: The **pileated woodpecker** has a red crest and a large black body about the size of a crow! It is really loud and it sounds like a drumroll while it is pecking away at a tree. It makes **huge oval holes** and is the second largest woodpecker in North America! You can call this bird either a **Pile-ee-ated or a Pill-ee-ated** woodpecker! Take your peck . . . we mean pick!

⓮

Find the Flat Rock Overlooking the Skyline Drive & Sit & Take a Break!

_____

10 POINTS

(Straight ahead---you can't miss it.)
SPECIAL HINT: Break time! If you have water, snacks, or a pillow . . . now would be the time to bring it out. Enjoy the view and the break!

⓯

Find the Short Rock Wall!

_____

10 POINTS

(To the right---below the flat rock viewpoint)
SPECIAL HINT: The **CCC boys** helped work on trails in Shenandoah and built bridges, walls, picnic grounds . . . and more. The CCC boys lived in camps run much like military camps, wore uniforms, and were paid about $30 each month. Twenty-five dollars of that was sent back home to help support their families.

⑯

Find the Oldest Rocks in the Entire National Park!

---

10 POINTS

(Stand on the flat boulder---look straight out---find the rocky mountain top---just behind a closer mountain.)

SPECIAL HINT: You are looking at **Old Rag** mountain. The boulders on this mountain are over **one billion years old!** The mountain looks "raggedy" from a distance. That is how it got its name, "Old Rag."

WE RECOMMEND YOU SIT HERE AWHILE AND ENJOY! AT HIKERS MUST REST TO MAKE IT THE WHOLE WAY! YOU ARE AN AT HIKER . . . SO FEEL FREE TO TAKE A BREAK BEFORE YOU HEAD BACK DOWN THE TRAIL TO THE PICNIC GROUNDS!

CONGRATULATIONS!

You have just completed a
SHENANDOAH NATIONAL PARK
SCAVENGER HIKE ADVENTURE!

Appalachian Trail Ridge Hike

10 Points for Each Item Found

TOTAL SCORE: _____

CERTIFIED ACHIEVEMENT LEVEL: _____

over **80** to **100** points: **City Slicker**

over **100** to **120** points: **Pioneer Scout**

over **120** points: **Frontier Explorer**

Name(s): _____

Witness(es) thereof: _____

_____

Date: _____

14
Scavenger Hike Adventure

MODERATE

3.4 MILES ROUNDTRIP

LESS THAN 3 HOURS

Riprap Trail to Calvary Rocks and Chimney Rock

Why This is a Great Trail! This is an amazing Scavenger Hike Adventure leading you to incredible **white quartzite rock overlooks** with **stunning views**! Quartzite rocks are mostly found in the southern part of the park and are about as special as special gets! This trail is called "**riprap**" and you will find plenty of it! You will find a **bench that continues to grow** and **views that are sure to knock your hiking socks off!** Find a high wall of milky white rocks with **500 million year old worm trails**, a deep crevice that once had a **bridge** over it . . . but no more . . . and signs of a **forest fire**. You will hike through areas that are officially designated as "**wilderness**" and you do need to be especially careful! After all, this is a wilderness Scavenger Hike Adventure!

Where's the Trail? This Scavenger Hike Adventure begins at **milepost 90** of the Skyline Drive in the South District of the park. Enter the Riprap parking lot on the west side of the drive. You will begin your hike on the Appalachian Trail for less than a half mile and then continue into the wilderness on Riprap Trail to Calvary Rocks and Chimney Rock!

About the Trail: This is a **MODERATE** trail that is not too easy, but definitely not too hard. You won't be real tired at the end, but then again you probably won't feel like doing jumping jacks either. Just when you think the trail is steep it will head down and then just when you think it is easy it will head uphill. There is a great overlook on the right of the trail with free front row seats to a beautiful view! A snack or lunch would be sure to "hit the spot" at this awesome white rocky overlook!

How Long is This Hike? This hike is **3.4 miles roundtrip**. Plan for it to take **less than 3 hours** with plenty of time to check out the views of Paine Run and the Shenandoah Valley.

Things To Hunt For

(Earn 10 points for each treasure you find.)

❶

Find the Sign that Welcomes Your Dog!

10 POINTS

(On the right of the trail)
SPECIAL HINT: Quick! Go back to Pennsylvania or New York or West Virginia and get "man's best friend"! You could have brought your 4-legged family member on this Scavenger Hike Adventure. There are **only about 10 trails in the park that dogs cannot hike on**.

BE SURE TO ALWAYS FOLLOW THE PARK RULES!

❷

Find the Appalachian Trail!

10 POINTS

(Look on the concrete marker to be sure you are on the Appalachian Trail.)
SPECIAL HINT: Yes, this is the famous *Appalachian Trail!* You will now head north on the AT for .4 mile before entering officially designated "**wilderness**" on Riprap Trail! Follow the white-painted rectangles (white blazes) on the trees! **White blazes** are painted on rocks and trees all the way from Georgia to Maine on the AT! Someone must have had a big bucket of paint!!

❸

Find the Signs of Fire along the Appalachian Trail!

10 POINTS

(On the right and left of the trail)
SPECIAL HINT: Look for **charred tree stumps** or fallen trees along the trail. Fires are a natural part of nature. In **October 1998** and again in **May 1999**, 2 big wildfires swept through this area.

❹
Find a Bench that Is Still Growing!

10 POINTS

(On the left side of trail---before you get to Riprap Trail)
SPECIAL HINT: Here is a perfect bench to "take a load off"! When is the last time you sat on a bench that was still growing? This tree's trunk grew sideways and then headed toward the sky! What an awesome tree!

❺
Find a Concrete Marker for Riprap Trail!

10 POINTS

(Ahead of you)
SPECIAL HINT: Follow Riprap Trail to the left 1 mile to **Calvary Rocks** and then you will hike on to **Chimney Rock**! You are now officially on Riprap Trail and are officially in designated **"wilderness."** Go on down!

❻
Find Lots of Fallen Dead Trees!

10 POINTS

(On both sides of the trail)
SPECIAL HINT: The forests in Shenandoah National Park have lots of **fallen trees**! **Hurricane winds, landslides, ice storms, and insects** take down trees each year. These dead trees are also an important part of the forest. They will become **homes for animals and insects** and even **give life to new plants** that will begin growing from dead stumps. Nothing is wasted out here in the wilderness.

❼
Find 2 Masts for an Old Ship!

10 POINTS

(One is on the left of the trail---and one is directly across from that tree---on the right of the trail---you will hike right between them.)
SPECIAL HINT: **White pine** trees have rough bark, soft green needles, and were used for sailing **masts** on big ships. **Indians** used the inner **bark** to **help treat a sore throat or cold.** What a tree!!! White pine trees have long, soft, green needles. The **needles** are in bundles or **packets of 5**. These beautiful trees add lots of green to the forest in the winter. They grow really fast and often **live 400 years**!

❽ Find Mountain Laurel Shrubs!

10 POINTS

(On the left and right of the trail--- especially as you go up the next hill) SPECIAL HINT: Find a shrub that has **leaves that are evergreen**, **smooth**, and **leathery** and *about* the **length of your finger**! The leaves are also a bit **shiny** and very shiny when wet. In the spring these shrubs are filled with large, beautiful **clusters of flowers**! They may be light pink, dark pink, reddish-pink, purplish-pink, or even white. In the spring, when the mountain laurel is in bloom, it often looks like you are hiking through a beautiful bouquet of flowers!

❾ Find Riprap!

10 POINTS

(Hike a while---if you don't turn right---you will run into it.) SPECIAL HINT: Find a mountainside of **broken stones covered with green lichen (pronounced LIKE-in).** This lichen looks like light green flaking paint but it is really a combination of **algae and fungus.** These broken stones are called **riprap**!

❿ Find an Awesome Lookout Point!

10 POINTS

(On the right of the trail) SPECIAL HINT: Someone will say, "Did we miss it?" Just tell them, "No, it's up ahead." These **cream-colored rocks** were once beach sand! They are called **Erwin quartzite**. An ocean once covered this area and these rocks were just part of the sand on the beach. If you see waves rolling in right now, you either passed through a time warp or took a wrong turn. Surf's up!

⑪

Find an Old Pitch Pine Tree!

10 POINTS

(On the trail---near the overlook---on the left)
SPECIAL HINT: This **pitch pine** tree has many, many branches and has very rough thick bark. Pioneers called this tree "**candlewood**" because the knots were burned as torches. The needles are in bundles or packets of 3.

⑫

Find Calvary Rocks & 500-Million-Year-Old Worm Trails!

10 POINTS

(On the left of the trail---look up.)
SPECIAL HINT: This high wall of quartzite rocks runs along the left side of the trail. Find either vertical **worm burrows** a little smaller than a pencil coming out of the rocks or small circles in the rocks much, much smaller than a penny. Remember how this was all once beach and ocean sand? Well, ancient worms burrowed into that sand before it became hardened quartzite. Those worms wiggled around here about **500 million years ago.**

⑬

Find a Favorite Snack of Flying Squirrels!

10 POINTS

(On large rocks---along the trail on the left and right)
SPECIAL HINT: Find something that looks like **dead leaves** on the rocks. This is **rock tripe** and flying squirrels just love to nibble on it! It is brown and black and when it gets wet it turns green.

⑭

Find Where a Bridge Used To Be!

10 POINTS

(Go downhill awhile---on the right of the trail---as the trail turns sharply left.)
SPECIAL HINT: *BE VERY CAREFUL* as you go to check out this overlook area. There are many *SHEER DROPS!!!* You have found **Chimney Rock!!!** To be sure you are at Chimney Rock, carefully look for iron pegs in the rocks that *used* to anchor the bridge that *used* to be here. Not any more!!!

⓯

Find a Safe Place To Sit!

——
10 POINTS

(On a solid flat rock---in a safe area)
SPECIAL HINT: *This is a dangerous spot if you are not careful!* Find a safe place to sit before trying to find #16.

⓰

Find Something Flying Without Flapping!

——
10 POINTS

(While sitting on a rock)
SPECIAL HINT: **Turkey vultures** have red bare heads, dark bodies, and they rarely flap their wings. They just glide around in the wind and soar over the mountains. Ahhhhh . . . to be a turkey vulture!

HEAD BACK THE WAY YOU CAME ON RIPRAP TRAIL!

FOLLOW THE BLUE BLAZES AND THE AT HEADING SOUTH BACK TO RIPRAP PARKING LOT!

READ THE SIGNS CAREFULLY SO YOU ARE SURE TO GO THE RIGHT WAY!!!

CONGRATULATIONS!

You have just completed a
SHENANDOAH NATIONAL PARK
SCAVENGER HIKE ADVENTURE!

Riprap Trail to Calvary Rocks & Chimney Rock

10 Points for Each Item Found
TOTAL SCORE: _____
CERTIFIED ACHIEVEMENT LEVEL: _____

over **80** to **100** points: **City Slicker**
over **100** to **120** points: **Pioneer Scout**
over **120** points: **Frontier Explorer**

Name(s):_____

Witness(es) thereof:_____

_____

Date:_____

Keep Exploring Shenandoah!

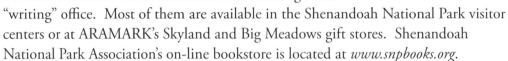

We listened to a lot of park rangers, former park resident descendants, and other locals to research the hidden treasures. Following is a list of some of our favorite books that were scattered about in our log cabin "writing" office. Most of them are available in the Shenandoah National Park visitor centers or at ARAMARK's Skyland and Big Meadows gift stores. Shenandoah National Park Association's on-line bookstore is located at *www.snpbooks.org*.

(TIP: IF YOU JOIN THE ASSOCIATION, YOU GET BIG DISCOUNTS ON BOOKS, MAPS AND VIDEOS AT THE VISITOR CENTERS, AND EVEN FOOD AT CONCESSIONER FACILITIES INSIDE THE PARK.)

Amberson, Joanne. *Easy Hikes on the Appalachian National Scenic Trail in Shenandoah National Park.* Shenandoah National Park Association, 2008.

------------. *Hikes to Peaks and Vistas in Shenandoah National Park.* Shenandoah National Park Association, 2006.

------------. *Short Hikes in Shenandoah National Park.* Shenandoah National Park Association, 2008.

------------. *Hikes to Waterfalls in Shenandoah National Park.* Shenandoah National Park Association, 2009.

------------. *The Fox Hollow Trail.* Shenandoah National Park Association, 2001.

Badger, Robert L. *Geology Along Skyline Drive.* Shenandoah National Park Association, 2004.

Barreda, Michael. *Circuit Hikes in Shenandoah National Park.* 15th Edition. Potomac Appalachian Trail Club, 2005.

Crandall, Hugh, and Reed L. Engle. *Shenandoah: The Story Behind the Scenery.* KC Publications, Inc., 2006.

Donovon, Amy. *Birds of Prey.* National Geographic Society, 2003.

Engle, Reed L. *The Greatest Single Feature . . . A Skyline Drive: 75 Years of a Mountaintop Motorway.* Shenandoah National Park Association, 2006.

------------. *Everything Was Wonderful: A Pictorial History of the Civilian Conservation Corps in Shenandoah National Park*. Shenandoah National Park Association, 1999.

------------. *In the Light of the Mountain Moon: An Illustrated History of Skyland*. Shenandoah National Park Association, 2003.

Evert, Laura. *Whitetail Deer*. NorthWord Press, 2000.

Feeney, Kathy. *Black Bears*. NorthWord Press, 2000.

Floyd, Tom. *Lost Trails and Forgotten People: The Story of Jones Mountain*. The Potomac Appalachian Trail Club, 2004.

Gildart, Bert and Jane. *Best Easy Day Hikes Shenandoah National Park*. Third Edition. Globe Pequot Press, 2006.

------------. *Hiking Shenandoah National Park*. Third Edition. Globe Pequot Press, 2006.

Hackley, Paul. *A Hiker's Guide to the Geology of Old Rag Mountain in Shenandoah National Park*. Shenandoah National Park Association, 2006.

Halfpenny, James C., and Jim Bruchac. *Scats and Tracks of the Mid-Atlantic*. Globe Pequot Press, 2002.

Horning, Audrey. *In the Shadow of Ragged Mountain: Historical Archeology of Nicholson, Corbin, and Weakley Hollows*. Shenandoah National Park Association, 2004.

Houk, Rose. *The Edge of the Sky: Shenandoah National Park Road Guide*. Sierra Press, 2006.

Lambert, Darwin. *Herbert Hoover's Hideaway*. Shenandoah National Park Association, 1971

------------. *The Undying Past of Shenandoah National Park*. Roberts Rinehart, 2001.

Lindsay, Terry and Patressa. *Birds of Shenandoah National Park*. Shenandoah National Park Association, 2005.

Lyle, Katie Letcher. *The Complete Guide to Edible Wild Plants, Mushrooms, Fruits, and Nuts*. The Lyons Press, 2004.

Manning, Russ. *75 Hikes in Virginia's Shenandoah National Park*. Second Edition. The Mountaineers, 2007.

Mazzeo, Peter M. *An Illustrated Guide to Ferns and Fern Allies of Shenandoah National Park*. Second Edition. Shenandoah National Park Association, 1981.

Nolen, Robyn. *Stony Man Trail*. Shenandoah National Park Association, 2004.

Peterson, Roger Tory. *Peterson First Guide to North American Birds*. Fourth Edition. Houghton Mifflin Company, 1986.

Plant, Ian J. *Shenandoah: Wonder and Light*. Mountain Trail Press, 2005.

Reeder, Carolyn, and Jack. *Shenandoah Secrets: The Story of the Park's Hidden Past*. The Potomac Appalachian Trail Club, 1998.

Simpson, Ann and Rob. *Born Wild in Shenandoah*. Farcountry Press, 2007.

The Potomac Appalachian Trail Club. *Appalachian Trail Guide to Shenandoah National Park. 13th Edition*. The Potomac Appalachian Trail Club, 2009.

Website Addresses

Shenandoah National Park (SNP): *www.nps.gov/shen*

Shenandoah National Park Association (SNPA): *www.snpbooks.org*

Leave No Trace: *www.LNT.org*

Wilderness: *www.wilderness.net*

ARAMARK (Park Concessioner): *www.visitshenandoah.com*

Potomac Appalachian Trail Club (PATC): *www.potomacappalachian.org*

Scavenger Hike Adventure Certificates: *www.scavengerhikeadventures.com*

Three Friends

Illustrator: G Webb

It is a special gift for us to call G Webb our friend, but it is a treasure to have him join us in our Scavenger Hike Adventures national park hiking series as artistic guide and illustrator. G Webb teaches Sunday School at a little country church by a creek, has created a beautiful vineyard (that looks more like a painting than a farm) and is an active leader and benefactor in his rural mountain community. Somehow he has also found the time to coach our high school tennis team and become a nationally renowned watercolour artist.

Even though he still drives a 1953 pick-up truck, he does have a website and you can visit him at *gwebbgallery.com* or at his old homestead gallery.

Shenandoah National Park Association

The Shenandoah National Park Association, a non-profit organization, was founded in 1950 and has been serving Shenandoah National Park since then. The mission of the Association is to support the interpretive and educational programs of the park. Profits from sales are used for this purpose.

One of the ways SNPA supports the park is by publishing books, pamphlets, and trail guides. We are especially pleased that SNPA published this guide. This and other items may be purchased in the park or on the website.

We highly recommend that you consider becoming a member of SNPA. For more information, or to purchase any items, visit the SNPA website at *www.snpbooks.org*.

ARAMARK

ARAMARK is the official park concessioner for the lodges, restaurants, waysides, gas stations, gift stores, stable, and laundry/shower units at Shenandoah National Park. The lodging and cabins inside the national park are a unique and special part of its history and ARAMARK is the caretaker of those properties.

NATIONAL PARK
VIRGINIA

We were honored when they asked us to research the history for each of the special historical cabins in Shenandoah and share their incredible stories of the past. You will find those stories posted inside the cabins.

We also created two special Scavenger Hike Adventures for Big Meadows and Skyland Resort to help guests explore and appreciate the hidden historical and natural "treasures" surrounding those two historic areas. They are available at Skyland Resort and Big Meadows Lodge.

SNPA and ARAMARK enthusiastically supported our new concept of *interactive hiking* and we consider it a privilege to partner with them in helping visitors explore and appreciate the majestic beauty and wonder of Shenandoah National Park.